My Family in
AMERICA
SINCE 1620

WILLIAM G. CARTER

iUniverse®

MY FAMILY IN AMERICA SINCE 1620

iUniverse books may be ordered through booksellers or by contacting:

iUniverse
1663 Liberty Drive
Bloomington, IN 47403
www.iuniverse.com
1-800-Authors (1-800-288-4677)

ISBN: 978-1-4917-8823-3 (sc)
ISBN: 978-1-4917-8824-0 (hc)
ISBN: 978-1-4917-8825-7 (e)

Library of Congress Control Number: 2016901330

Print information available on the last page.

iUniverse rev. date: 02/26/2016

Chapter 1

MY MOTHER'S FAMILY ARRIVES IN AMERICA IN 1620

O N MY MOTHER'S SIDE OF the family, I am a descendant of William Brewster. He was born in 1566 in Wales, which is a part of the United Kingdom. He would become my great-grandfather, with several more "greats" added, of course. He was an elder of his church in Scrooby, England, and attended Cambridge University. His neighbors and friends were aware of the new land of America, and William Brewster became one of the key leaders of the Mayflower expedition.

The Mayflower group left England on September 6, 1608. They moved across the channel to Holland, where they could safely plan their trip across the Atlantic Ocean to the new land of freedom that would later become the United States of America. Word was spreading about the new country and the vast areas available for peaceful settlement. There was work to be done and money to be raised before they would be able to set sail.

One hundred and two men, women, and children, along with the necessary crew, boarded the Mayflower in Holland in early 1620. Their wind-powered trip across the Atlantic was under way. The voyage took a little longer than two months. On November 9, 1620, they arrived in North America at the tip of Cape Cod peninsula. After two days of exploration, they chose the site on which they would establish their colony.

The Mayflower Compact was prepared and signed by the forty-one men on board on November 11, 1620. Historians have recognized the Mayflower Compact as the first official government document created in America. It stated the rules by which they would live peacefully in their new colony. My great-grandfather (with many more greats added of course) Brewster was the scribe, or secretary, of this group, and he would have had a major influence on the creation of the famous Mayflower Compact.

The first five who signed the compact were John Carver, William Bradford, Isaac Allerton, Edward Winslow, and William Brewster. I am proud to proclaim that I am a descendant of William Brewster who was instrumental in the preparation of that officially recognized document.

By springtime of 1621 many of the colonists had died from tuberculosis and other diseases. In April 1644, they celebrated an event that would become known as the first Thanksgiving Day in America. They were giving thanks for their successful arrival in this land where they could live peacefully and in security. The Mayflower Colony would later be known as the Massachusetts Bay Colony. America was vast open country at that time, and they were living off the fruits of the land. There were no stores or shops as we know them today for purchasing food or family supplies.

An entire book has been written about William Brewster's life: *Pilgrim, A Biography of William Brewster.* The author of that book is Mary B. Sherwood who is also a descendant of William Brewster. Her book is more than two hundred pages and beautifully done. There are photographs of artists' renditions of how Brewster would have appeared. The Library of Congress is another good source for information on the Mayflower.

In the early days of the Mayflower Colony, the Native Americans were friendly and helpful. When I visited the site, the original log cabins had rotted away. However, some modern cabins had been constructed to depict the original homes. As I walked this site of one of the first colonies in America, I tried to imagine what life would have been like there in 1621 for my ancestor William Brewster.

More ships were arriving and more colonies were being established. They would soon join to form the original thirteen colonies. The total number of immigrants living in America in 1620 has been reported at about 4,100. After four years the Mayflower Colony would have a population of about 250. Today, the Mayflower arrival site is known as Plymouth, Massachusetts. I was very excited when I personally visited this site, knowing that I was walking the area where my own ancestor William Brewster had lived in the 1620s. He passed away in 1644.

Chapter 2

MORE EARLY HISTORY ON MY MOTHER'S FAMILY

OTHER NOTABLE INDIVIDUALS ON MY mother's side of the family include Benjamin Mayberry Prentiss, a descendant of William Brewster. He was born in Belleville, Virginia, in 1819 and became an auctioneer and a rope maker. Rope was a product in major demand at that time in history.

Also, Daniel Kober and family arrived from Germany in 1730 in what would later become the Philadelphia area. The name was eventually changed to *Cover*, pronounced with a hard *C*. The Daniel Cover family would have a son, James Harvey Cover, and he would become my great-grandfather.

The Cover family was based in Maryland in the early 1800s. The westward movement in America was under way, and members of the Cover family moved on westward to Illinois and then to northwest Missouri in 1883. James Harvey Cover became publisher of the *Albany Ledger* newspaper.

The next family move was to Bethany, Missouri, a few miles to the east. There Mr. Cover began publishing the *Bethany Broad Axe* newspaper which was later changed to the *Bethany Democrat*. He published it for ten years. He would later sell that operation and open a furniture store in Bethany. That was successful for a number of years, and then he sold the business and served as assistant doorkeeper of the House of Representatives in Washington, DC. In 1900, he and his wife, Margaret, moved back to Missouri.

James Harvey Cover would have a son, James Wilbert Cover; in his adult life he was known as J. W. Cover. He married Mary Prentiss, the daughter of Benjamin Prentiss of Civil War fame, and they had a daughter in 1896. This was Leah Cover, and she would grow to adulthood and marry William Y. Carter, an ancestor of the leader of the Carter Wagon Train in 1841. I am the fourth child of William and Leah Carter, born in 1929. Others in the Cover family included Albert, Donald, Frank, Fred, Rodney, and Norma.

Chapter 3

THE CARTER WAGON
TRAIN TO MISSOURI, 1841

L IKE THE BREWSTERS, THE CARTER family came from Wales. I have no record of the precise time of their arrival in America, but we do know that Levi Carter and his wife, Susanna, were living in Tennessee in the mid-1700s and that they would become my great-great-great-great grandparents. They had a son named Elijah, and he married into the Glendenning family, which had arrived from Scotland. Elijah Carter became my great-grandfather (with more "greats" added). Then into that family, my own grandfather Adam Carter was born in 1872, just thirty-one years after the arrival of the Carter Wagon Train in Missouri. He was the son of William Glendenning Carter.

In the 1830s and 1840s, wagon trains were starting the major expansion westward into the open virgin land available for settlement in America. In 1841, the Distribution-Preemption Act declared that land legally open for settlement. That same year, the Carter family journeyed from eastern Indiana westward through Illinois and into Missouri, which had become the twenty-fourth state in America in 1821. The wagon train's trip would have been approximately eight hundred miles.

The wagons were horse drawn. The first horses had been brought to the United States in the 1500s and 1600s; motor-driven vehicles did not become available until the late 1800s. When I drove the approximate route that the Carter Wagon Train had followed from Indiana to Missouri, I tried to imagine what it would have been like to travel that far in a horse-drawn wagon.

That was quite simple for me to understand, for I'd spent many years on our farm harnessing and driving our team of horses, which provided the power to pull wagons or other farm equipment six days a week. Based on my early life on the farm, I calculated that it would have taken two to three months to complete that lengthy journey. They had to stop at least three times a day to give the horses a break and to provide a midday meal for all.

If there was a stormy day, they would have had to stop and wait for reasonable weather. Many were walking ahead and alongside the wagons as they made their way along. There were no roads to follow. The country was just open land with only a few local trails.

Scouts walked or rode on horseback out ahead to find the best route to travel. They had to avoid excessively wooded areas and find the best place to cross the rivers and streams. Once the scouts had found the appropriate route to follow, one would return and lead the wagon train while the others continued the search ahead.

In the 1840s, my home state of Missouri was on the western border of the United States. Kansas City became officially incorporated in 1853, twelve years after the Carter Wagon Train arrived. This great land of America was still in its very early years of development. The Carter Wagon Train would have consisted of two or three wagons per family. By one early report, there were about forty wagons on that journey. They were transporting not only family members but also all necessary household items.

This is an artist's drawn image of a covered wagon of the 1840s.

The Carter Wagon Train arrival site is about midway between the current towns of Albany and Bethany in northwest Missouri. The leader of this wagon train was my great-great-grandfather, Elijah Carter. There were also members of the Glendenning family. Elijah Carter's son, William Glendenning Carter, was born in a covered wagon before they had completed construction of their first log cabin.

They had to saw down trees with a hand-drawn crosscut saw and then saw them into the proper-size logs to stack and build the cabins. At that time, there were wild animals roaming the country. Through domestication and careful breeding, these wild animals would become the fine cattle, horses and other livestock that we have on farms today. The same was probably true for chickens, ducks, and turkeys.

The arrival site of the Carter Wagon Train in Missouri would become Gentry County in 1845. The adjoining county to the east is Harrison County, which also was organized in 1845. The old original county courthouse in Bethany burned in January of 1874, and a new brick building was constructed. The growing Carter families would move on throughout the area. My grandfather Adam Carter would eventually establish his farm just to the north of what is now New Hampton, Missouri.

An artist's drawing of an early log cabin of the 1840s

The early settlers were using what was known as split rail fences. They would chop down trees from the plentiful supply in wooded areas and then stack the logs and limbs from those trees to construct their fences as well as their log cabins. At this time in the early 1840s, Missouri is reported to have been the eighth state in size and the fifth in population in America. Where the Carter Wagon Train arrived is about one hundred miles to the northeast of Kansas City, which was only a village in the 1840s. It would not become an incorporated town until 1853.

Today, Kansas City, Missouri, is the largest city in the state of Missouri, with a population of 466,600. Couple that with neighboring Kansas City, Kansas, bordering immediately to the west with a population of 48,500, and you have a major metropolitan area with a population well over 500,000.

In the 1800s, there was only one way to build a place to call home: chop down trees from the wooded areas. After that was done, the logs were trimmed and then stacked properly to build a log cabin. At this time in history, middle America and westward was open land ready for the increasing population to arrive. All settlers had to do was carefully stake out their own tract of approximately one hundred acres, take that information to an office in a nearby village, and record it as their own tract of land. I recall from very early family conversations that there was about a ten-dollar charge to make this registration. That was a substantial amount of money at that time in history.

After completing their journey in 1841, the Glendenning family, which had been part of the Carter Wagon Train, built a church and a school for the growing community. The Carter Cemetery was also established. I have walked through that historic cemetery. It was obvious that gravestones of that early era were not the granite markers of today. They were constructed of concrete, and many had deteriorated to the point of leaning or falling over and were unreadable as to who was buried there. Some were replaced in later years with permanent granite gravestones. This includes the gravestones for my great-great-grandfather Elijah Carter, his son William Glendenning Carter, and their families.

My great-grandfather William Glendenning Carter served in World War I, which took place from 1914 to 1918. He later established a bank in a nearby village just a few miles from where the Carter Wagon Train arrived. Family records reveal that he then moved a few miles to New Hampton, where he became involved in the early development of a lumber company. Small towns were being established to stock supplies needed by the increasing number of early settlers in the Midwest.

The farm where I would later live was a few miles to the east of the Carter Wagon Train arrival site. There was a stream flowing through our 160-acre farm called Long Branch Creek. There was only one small sturdy bridge on that creek. It was the only place a horse-drawn wagon or a tractor could cross. In my early grade-school years, I would take my shoes and socks off and wade across that flowing creek. Occasionally, when there had been considerable rainfall, the water flowing was at a depth and speed too dangerous to wade into.

Therefore, I can understand why the Carter Wagon Train scouts had to constantly search for the best and safest route to follow in order to avoid heavily forested areas and to find the best place to cross rivers and streams. This was before roads and highways were available.

Their major challenge would have been crossing the Mississippi River. There were no bridges across major rivers at that time in history. We know that they camped out for about a week on the eastern edge of the Mississippi to carefully locate the safest place to cross. Then they had to make special plans to prepare for crossing on westward into Missouri. The wagon train was successful in crossing the mighty Mississippi River.

As I drove the approximate route that they would have been traveling and came to the Mississippi River, I tried to envision what it would have been like for them to cross it in wagons. For additional reference, it was not until 1865 that the US mail system was created and Pony Express mail delivery was under way. The first gasoline-powered automobile did not become available until 1886. That was only ten years before my mother and father were born.

I have walked through much of the area where the Carter Wagon Train arrived in 1841, trying to envision what daily life was like for my family there in the 1840s. My own early life was spent on our nearby farm, so I could pretty well imagine what life was like for them at that time in history. There would have been a lot of horseback riding to do in order to maintain contact with neighbors and friends.

Chapter 4

MORE INFORMATION ON MY EARLY CARTER FAMILY HISTORY

M Y GRANDFATHER, ADAM CARTER, WAS born in 1872, thirty-one years after the arrival of the Carter Wagon Train in Missouri. He was the son of William Glendenning Carter, who was the one born in the covered wagon. Adam Carter married Frances Young, and their family included William, Edgar, Tommy, Raymond, and Velma. William grew up there in northwest Missouri and married Leah Cover, a descendant of William Brewster of Mayflower fame.

I was born to William and Leah Carter in 1929. There was some thought of giving me the name William Glendenning Carter in honor of my great-grandfather Carter. However, after some consideration, my parents decided on keeping the *G* but making it William Gerald Carter. Therefore, when I sign my name today as William G. Carter, the memory of my great-grandfather William Glendenning Carter often comes to mind.

Moving now to rural life for the Carter family in northwest Missouri, it would have been nothing like farm life today. Their source of power for cultivation of fields for crop planting was horses, before cars and tractors were available. When I was in my grade-school years in the early and mid-1930s, Dad was still using his historic old single plow when it was time to plow our small garden.

You could get much closer to the fence line with that little plow than with tractor-drawn plows. Back in the early 1800s, that would have been the method of plowing ground when the large fields were being prepared for crop planting. With the strength of your own hands, you would adjust the front part of that plow properly into the ground and walk along behind as a team of horses pulled it through the field or garden.

It was in the early 1930s that farm tractors came into general use. My father had purchased one of the first tractors sold in our neighborhood in northwest Missouri but he was still using his relic old single horse drawn plow to begin preparation of our small garden for planting. When tractors became available in the 1930s, our tractor drawn double plow was being utilized to prepare all fields for crop planting.

Before I started first grade in 1934, I was beginning to observe what farm life was like. After plowing the field, next came our tractor-drawn disk. It further broke the chunky plowed soil into proper condition. Then the harrow would be drawn through the field with a team of horses to further break up the chunks of dirt. Now the soil was ready for planting.

We had battery-powered flashlights on the farm. They had been invented and came into use in 1903 when my father was seven years old. Electricity first came into use in 1879, but for families out in the country at that time, there were no electric lines. It was just the glass bowl lamps that could be lighted by striking a match and holding it just above the very small special heavy cloth material that was now soaked with kerosene. This created a small constant flame protected by the glass chimney placed on top of the lamp. That was the method of lighting in our house before electricity was available in rural America.

We also had kerosene-burning lanterns for use out on the farm after dark when necessary. These were less sophisticated than the kerosene-fueled lamps in the house. There was an occasional need to check cows having a calf or other nighttime livestock activity requiring immediate attention.

The very early county office buildings in the 1840s would have been log cabins. In addition to their own log cabins, the settlers were building log-cabin schools and churches. At this point in history, there were vast areas of open virgin land available for claim and settlement in the United States.

Kansas City, Missouri was still a small town with a population of about 10,000 when the Carter family arrived and established their log-cabin homes in 1841. Soon would come commercial buildings that, while constructed of bricks rather than logs, bore no resemblance to the commercial structures of today.

This is the original brick county courthouse in Bethany, Missouri.

Immigrants were still pouring into the United States at this time in history, and early settlers had to continue moving into the virgin open land in the west that was available for settlement. The town of Bethany, relatively close to the site of the Carter Wagon Train's arrival in Missouri, was incorporated in 1845, just four years after the wagon train's arrival.

On my first visit to the Carter arrival site, there was still a log cabin standing. It was terribly decayed. I can understand why, for even in my early days on the farm, it was obvious that if you did not keep a building painted, it would rot away. That log cabin is no longer there.

The Carter family continued to grow, and this would have required building more log cabins in the mid-1800s. I have walked throughout the wagon train arrival site visualizing what life would have been like for my great-grandparents in rural America at that time. Food supply came from the land. There were wild native fruit trees and other growth that could be utilized for daily food.

The settlers started cultivating and planting their gardens and crops on the soil of what was now their home. Small towns were springing up, and the Midwest population was increasing. Farm equipment was still in the early stages of development, far from the modern equipment of today.

On our farm in northwest Missouri in the early 1930s, we devoted some time each day to chopping down the weeds growing around the vegetables in our garden. I spent time almost every day helping Dad and Mom with the garden work in my early grade-school years. Back in the 1840s, there was no quick trip to a nearby grocery store to purchase canned fruits and vegetables or other needs in the log cabin kitchen. Their daily food supply came from their backyard garden.

Communication by daily mail service in the United States was under way in 1891. In its annual report of 1899, the postal service announced that it had tested the practicality of using the newly invented automobile for mail delivery. By that statement, we know that mail delivery prior to that was by horseback or horse-drawn buggy. My own great-grandparents and grandparents experienced the earliest days of US mail delivery.

Chapter 5

MY GREAT-GRANDFATHER BENJAMIN MAYBERRY PRENTISS AND HIS EXPERIENCE IN THE CIVIL WAR

STUDYING AMERICAN HISTORY WAS INTERESTING for me in high school and college. It was even more personal and exciting when I read the history of my great-grandfather Benjamin Mayberry Prentiss. He was on my mother's side of the family.

Benjamin Prentiss was born in Belleville, Virginia. The family joined the westward movement in the 1700s, establishing their home in Illinois. They moved on westward to Missouri when Benjamin was seventeen years old.

In 1847, when Benjamin was in his early adulthood, he began the practice of law. He had not attended college, but he was an intelligent scholar. This would have been typical of many citizens of that era. Our education infrastructure was still in its earliest stages.

In 1860, Benjamin Prentiss ran for an elected position in the US House of Representatives. He was not successful. His first wife, Margaret Lodousky, passed away in 1862 and he later married Mary Worthington Whitney. From these two marriages would come twelve children, and one of the daughters would become my grandmother on my mother's side of the family.

Benjamin Prentiss served in the Illinois militia during the Mexican-American war early in the 1860s. He recruited and organized a company of volunteers and was their captain. There was conflict as to just where the border should be between Mexico and the United States. It took a relatively brief war to resolve that problem.

Then in August of 1861, the war between the Northern and Southern states began—the Civil War. Benjamin Prentiss entered that war as an officer in the army of the North. First he received orders to join Ulysses S. Grant's Army in Tennessee. His unit was the sixth division.

My Great Grand Father Benjamin Prentiss

The historic Battle of Shiloh was fought in 1862 in Harden County, Tennessee. Benjamin Prentiss has been declared in historic documents as "the Hero of the Battle of Shiloh" for the army of the North. That battle site is now the Shiloh National Military Park.

It has been estimated that about 700,000 American lives were lost in the Civil War. That is more than any other war in the history of the United States. When I visited this battle site it personalized all that I had studied about the Civil War in high school and in college. Following are details of the Battle of Shiloh as explained to me personally by my official battle-site guide as I walked the area where that battle was fought.

General Prentiss and his fellow soldiers were carrying single-shot rifles with a metal barrel into which a bullet would be dropped. This was the weapon of the Civil War. There were two opposing lines of soldiers for each side. After the frontline soldier had fired his one-shot rifle, he would exchange places with the soldier just behind him who now had his weapon loaded and ready to fire. My official guide demonstrated the rifle-loading process for rifles of that era.

The soldier would set the rifle butt on the ground and then pour a small amount of gunpowder down the barrel from a packet he carried. After that, a bullet would be dropped down the rifle barrel. Then with a small rod, the soldier stuffed the bullet into place in the powder. The-one shot rifle was now loaded and ready to fire.

With the trigger pull, there would be a spark that ignited the powder, and that would send the bullet out the rifle barrel. The soldier would again exchange places with the soldier just behind him who now had his one-shot weapon reloaded and ready to fire. This was the method of battle during the Civil War, the battle between the Southern and Northern states. It was two lines of soldiers for each side exchanging places with one another constantly during battle.

During the first day of the Battle of Shiloh, troops for the North were arriving from a site just a few miles to the north on the Tennessee River where they were receiving one week of training. After that, they were floated a short distance downstream and would depart the boat very near the battle site. The boat would then be pulled back upriver by teams of horses on the riverbanks. Keep in mind that this was long before motorized equipment was available. Barge after barge of soldiers had to be floated downstream to the battle site.

At the training site, the soldiers were each issued a weapon. They had to learn the process of loading, firing, and then reloading their one-shot rifle. At that time in history, few if any had ever had a rifle in his possession before. At that time, General Prentiss and his unit had been issued an order to "hold at all hazards until sundown." They knew that the army of the South was progressing northward.

Additional troops for the army of the North arrived at battle site throughout the night. It was one barge of soldiers being floated down river to battle site at a time. As explained by my Shiloh battle site guide, it took several barge-loads of soldiers to bring the defensive unit to a safe number. After sundown, when nighttime was fast approaching, the fighting would stop. The barge-by-barge transfer of troops from upstream would continue throughout the night after the first day of the Battle of Shiloh.

During combat, soldiers had to be in plain sight of the opposing line of the enemy for their one-shot trigger pull. On the first day of battle, units to Prentiss's right and to his left retreated. He was the commanding colonel for his unit and they were nearly surrounded by the larger number of approaching Southern soldiers.

He had no choice but to retreat to a sunken road area where he allowed his men to lay on the ground and then fire and reload their one-shot rifle as the opposing forces approached. Keep in mind that I did not learn this from history books. It was being personally explained and demonstrated to me by my official guide on my visit to the site. At nightfall, General Prentiss had no choice but to surrender. His men were out of ammunition and virtually surrounded.

At daylight the next day, Prentiss and his men were being escorted off southward to prison. However, additional units had arrived during the night from upstream on the Tennessee River and soon they would be successful in beginning their slow advance to the south. Eventually these units reached the site where Prentiss and his men were being held. They were now free.

After about a week of rehab time Benjamin Prentiss was promoted to the rank of major general for his success and courage throughout that period of the Civil War. He was placed in command of a unit that was stationed along the Mississippi River on the eastern border of Arkansas. General Prentiss is reported to have had approximately 20,000 men in this unit.

Soon would come the Battle of Helena. Just a short time before this battle would occur many of his men were transferred to another location leaving him with only about 4,000 soldiers. However, after intensive early conflict, Prentiss and his men were successful. The opposing forces retreated. This battle occurred in July of 1863.

General Prentiss and his men then moved on to Little Rock, Arkansas which is approximately 100 miles on to the west. Keep in mind that this was well before trucks and cars were in use. It was all feet on the ground or riding in horse-drawn wagons. At the battle of Little Rock, Prentiss and his men were once again successful for the Northern army. I have also visited this battle site.

The Civil War that started in 1861 came to an end in May of 1865. This historic war between the Northern and Southern states was necessary to keep the United States of America together as one nation with liberty and justice for all. I am now a great-grandfather myself and am very proud of the accomplishments of my own great-grandfather, Benjamin Mayberry Prentiss in this historic period of American history.

Chapter 6

BENJAMIN PRENTISS AND HIS LIFE AFTER THE CIVIL WAR

S OON AFTER THE CIVIL WAR, Benjamin Prentiss and his family moved to Quincy, Illinois where they lived until 1879. During this time in Illinois he became acquainted with Abraham Lincoln. Soon the Prentiss family moved on to Kirksville in northeast Missouri. There he traveled extensively by horse and wagon throughout the area marketing his rope products which were in great demand at that time in history.

Family records state that Benjamin Prentiss was invited to accept a governmental appointment in Washington, DC. He considered the possibility but made the decision that he did not want to make the move. He was then asked by President Benjamin Harrison to fill the position of postmaster in Bethany in northwest Missouri. He accepted and spent the remainder of his life with family and friends in Bethany.

My mother told stories of how her grandfather Prentiss would sing songs to her when she was a very young girl sitting on his lap. During a recent visit with family in Bethany, we drove to the site of the house that had been the Benjamin Prentiss home after the Civil War. It was interesting for me to take a quick walk in that historic neighborhood where my famous great-grandfather Prentiss had lived.

In the Bethany newspaper in 1995, there was an article on Benjamin Prentiss and his life in Bethany. It mentions that the Benjamin Prentiss Park had just been dedicated and it includes a family photograph of my sister Wilma Jean and her husband, Dean Murray onsite for the occasion. Their home is nearby. Other family members in the photo are Wilma Jean's daughter Joyce; my brother Robert Carter and his wife Helen; and my mother's youngest brother, Rodney Cover.

When Benjamin Prentiss passed away in 1901, the Missouri Legislature passed a resolution that reads as follows:

> **On the pages of history his name will appear as one on whose bravery and indomitable courage hung the fate of the Shiloh Battle and perhaps the Nation. He was a man who knew what was right and dared to tell it as he believed it.**

These facts and quotations from history make me proud to be a great-grandson of Benjamin Prentiss. I was born well after he passed away in Bethany, Missouri, but the kind and loving comments I remember my mother making about him are precious memories for me.

I have in my possession today a rocking chair that Benjamin Prentiss personally carved and constructed from a cherry tree that was growing in the backyard of his house in Bethany. Every time I look at that hand-constructed chair I am reminded of my famous great-grandfather. According to my mother, when he passed away many gathered at the Bethany Methodist Church to pay their final tribute. I have sat quietly on the benches of that church to visualize the funeral service that was held for Benjamin Prentiss.

Chapter 7

MY OWN EARLY LIFE ON OUR FIRST FARM IN NORTHWEST MISSOURI

W E GO FORWARD IN TIME to the very early years for me on our farm, which was located not far from where the Carter Wagon Train arrived in 1841. I was born in 1929, when Dr. Harned in Bethany was making house calls. One cold January morning, when reached by telephone and advised that a baby would soon arrive, he drove to our farmhouse, stayed overnight, and assisted in my delivery. This comes from family files, of course, which also verify that my older brother, Robert, and sisters Wilma Jean and Marian were also born on this farm.

This was well before electricity was available for those living in rural America. A dollar at that time in history would have been equal to about eighteen dollars today. We had a nice country home with a front living room, a downstairs bedroom for Mom and Dad, and a dining room and kitchen. Mom was Leah and Dad was William. Up an open stairway, there were three bedrooms for the children.

We had a wood burning stove in the front room of the house for heating and another in the kitchen for meal preparation. My memories begin in 1931 when I was two years old. In the winter months, when I would toddle down our open stairway in the morning, Dad would be getting the fire in the kitchen and front-room stoves going. The outside winter temperature at that time in northern Missouri could be well below zero.

One cold winter morning, Dad was sitting beside the stove in the front room making sure that all was well. When I arrived, he popped me up on his knee, and with a happy smile on his face, he asked his usual morning question: "Well, Sonny, how old are you?"

He had taught me the procedure of holding up two fingers on my right hand when I was two years old and mumbling "two." But this day, with a big smile on his face, he grabbed my hand just right and gave it a flip. A third finger popped up, and with a happy voice he emphatically said, "No, Gerald, this is your birthday. You are three years old." And that was the most memorable birthday of my entire life. That would have been in January of 1932.

When I was five years old, I began to learn how to drive our large steel-wheeled Farmal tractor. In the simplest of farm duties, I would be sitting on the tractor seat between Dad's knees with my hands on the vertical steering wheel when he was doing the tractor driving. I did not realize it then, but this was how he was teaching me to drive that tractor.

There was just one way to get this early tractor started, and that was with the hand crank. It would be placed into the very low front part of the tractor. Then you would turn the crank around and around, up and down, and that would get the tractor motor running. I was too young to do the cranking procedure, but I was learning the farming operation by observation and participating in the very simplest of duties.

I learned the tractor gears of first, second, third, and reverse. We had a large wooden gate from the barn lot out into the nearby pasture. This required Dad to stop, get down from the tractor, and open the gate. He would return to the tractor to drive it on through and stop to come back and shut the gate.

One day, when Dad stopped at the gate and as usual got down to open it, for the first time he called back to me, "Okay, Sonny, drive it on through. Don't pull the gas lever down, just let it idle on through."

I did so with great care, reaching way down to the clutch with my left foot to get the tractor into first gear. Now I was for the first time driving that Farmal tractor all by myself. It is one of the most vivid memories of my life. To me, that tractor was huge.

Our 1930 Farmal Tractor

I continued to learn a bit more tractor driving year by year, even though I was still not strong enough to be doing it out in the fields Dad was preparing for planting. I helped with the most simple farm chores. One of my first duties was to gather the eggs from the bottom row of nests in our chicken house when Dad was bringing in the feed and water for the chickens.

I could reach the bottom row of nests, and I put the eggs carefully in my little gallon bucket. As soon as possible, Dad would join me with his larger bucket and complete the egg-gathering from the upper row of nests. By observation and simple participation, I was learning the entire chicken-feeding and egg-gathering process.

A few years later, I would be tall enough to reach the top row of nests, so now I was doing the entire egg-gathering from both rows. As I grew older, in my preteen years, I would feed the chickens and gather the eggs all by myself. I was learning more simple farm duties year by year, helping Dad, Mom, and my brother, Robert, in the garden. My older sisters, Wilma Jean and Marian, helped Mom in the kitchen and with other household duties, as well as in the garden.

Sunday was dress-up day after morning chores were completed. It was time to get cleaned and bathed and ready for the short drive to the

Methodist church in nearby Martinsville. No fieldwork was done on Sunday. All we did was the necessary morning and evening farm chores.

Every morning, Monday through Saturday, the team of horses was brought to the barn and harnessed to be ready as needed during the day. The first team of horses that I remember was named Ball and Jim. Relatively soon in my early grade-school years, I drove that team of horses on regular farm duties when Dad was nearby. Then, as the months passed, more simple tractor-driving experiences came my way. Dad was carefully teaching me the farm duties that I would move on to year by year.

This was in the early 1930s. We would drive to the nearby small town of Martinsville there in northwest Missouri every week in our 1928 Pontiac to take our cream and eggs to the store. There would be a slip of paper delivered to the cash register stating the value of the cream and eggs and that would be balanced with grocery purchases. This would usually result in a modest check for us. It was not our major farm income but it did provide the necessary dollars for weekly purchase of grocery items.

Before we headed back to the farm from the Martinsville store it was often necessary to stop at the Beeks Service Station and fill the car with gasoline. Our first farm was to the south of Martinsville, which was first known as Middleton. The name was changed to Martinsville in 1872. That would have been the approximate year when my grandparents were born.

In the early 1870s, Martinsville is reported to have had a population of about two hundred residents. In the book *History of Missouri Illustrated*, there are more details on the early history of Martinsville, including information on physicians, stores, and merchants back in the 1800s. That was when this country town had considerably more residents than the years when I was living on our nearby farm in the early 1930s.

In my own early years, I remember the John Graham store on the north side of the street that passed through Martinsville. There was also a small restaurant on the south side of the street and a very small post office building serving not only the residents there but also the sizable surrounding rural area.

We did not have a heater or air conditioner in our 1928 Pontiac when I was just a kid in the early 1930s. That car was soon replaced with a 1929 Chevrolet and then a 1933 Chevrolet. Next came a 1935 Chevrolet, and then our 1938 Chevrolet. This was still the early years of automobiles, and they did not last nearly as long as cars of today.

My father, who was born in 1898, had learned the necessary farming skills from his father, Adam Carter. Before tractors came into general use in farming communities in the early 1900s, all power for pulling wagons and other farm equipment was provided by teams of horses. It could be two horses or four horses together pulling the larger farm equipment.

My Carter family history covers a period of early rural development from pioneer America in the early 1800s on into the early industrial age. A reunion of the Carter and Glendenning families was held in the late 1890s near the site where the family wagon train had arrived. This would have included my Grandfather and Grandmother Carter, and she had ancestors in the Glendenning family who had also arrived with the wagon train of 1841.

As a point of reference, it was in 1893 that the first successful gasoline-powered tractors and cars were built. This further identifies the approximate time in history when equipment became available to convert logs into lumber and the small wooden shingles used for roofing. Log cabins became history.

I recall seeing a log cabin that remained in the area where the Carter Wagon Train had arrived. That log cabin is no longer there. It was located near the historic Carter Cemetery where my great grandfather and his father, the leader of the Carter Wagon Train, are interred.

I have a family photo that shows my father sitting on his father's knee. He was the first child of Adam and Frances Carter and appears to be about two years old. That verifies that this photo was taken in about 1898 for Dad was born in 1896. There is also a bearded gentleman on the front row of that photo who would have been my great-grandfather William Glendenning Carter. He was the one born in the covered wagon before they had completed their first log cabin there in northwest Missouri.

My ancestors enjoyed the successful early growth and development of the United States in the 1800s. When I was studying American history in high school from 1942 to 1946 all these historical facts became quite personal for me relative to my own family in America from the landing of the Mayflower in 1620 and on to the Carter Wagon Train to Missouri in 1841.

Chapter 8

MORE FARM MEMORIES FOR ME IN THE 1930S

O N OUR FIRST FARM WE did not live on a graveled road. It was a dirt road. Dad had a special piece of equipment called a road drag that he would pull up and down our dirt road with the tractor to keep the roadway in the best possible condition. If we had enough rain to make it wet and slippery, the solution was to wait until sunshine came and dried the road.

It was on this first farm, when I was six years old, that I learned how to milk a cow. We had a very gentle cow named Old Red. While Dad and older brother Robert would be doing the real cow milking, I would be sitting on my own milk stool with a small bucket on the ground, struggling with the milking process. That was the only milk cow we ever had who was so gentle that you could set a bucket on the ground and continue with the hand-milking procedure.

That was not the way Robert and Dad were doing the milking. They were each sitting on a milk stool holding a three-gallon milk bucket between their knees—standard milking procedure. I was too young for that. Still, with my little hands, I could get at least a little bit of milk in the bucket. This cow was unusual, for she would never move. It is normal for a cow to move about a bit during the milking procedure.

After Dad had milked a couple of cows, he would come and properly complete the milking process for me. My hands were not yet large enough and strong enough to complete the job. Several months later I did move on to completing the milking job.

Year by year, I added another cow or two to my milking schedule. When I was in my later grade-school years and much stronger, I could almost keep up with Dad in the milking process. Soon Robert was out doing other farm chores while Dad and I completed the cow milking.

In the winter months in north Missouri, the snow on the country roadways would sometimes be excessive. It was necessary to wait until a somewhat warmer day arrived to melt the snow. A major winter snowstorm would build large drifts of snow that had to be personally scooped off the dirt road. Then the large heavy road drag would be pulled along, removing more snow. That would make our dirt road fairly passable.

Dad was also utilizing that road drag quite frequently to keep the roadway near our farm in comfortable travel condition. A rainstorm would make that dirt road too muddy for a few days for automobile travel.

Winter travel was sometimes a challenge. I recall a few times when Dad just hitched the horse team to the wagon and drove them to Martinsville to get the necessary weekly shopping done in the winter. This was likewise necessary on rare occasions during a very rainy week in the summer as well. We must keep in mind that at this time, in the early 1930s, it was still early history for automobiles.

At that time to start a car you turned the switch on and then put your foot on the starter. A gentle push down would normally get the car started. The starter was on the floor just to the left of the clutch, beside the brake pedal. With the car started and the motor running, you would push the clutch pedal down with your left foot and shift into first gear. Upon releasing the clutch to normal position, you started slowly moving. When you had speeded up just a little, it was time to shift into second gear, and the speed would increase slightly. Then it was another shift into third gear through the same process, and you were now traveling at a safe moderate speed down the road. We called the forward gears low, second, and high rather then first, second, and third.

When I was two years old I recall sitting on my mother's lap in the front seat of our 1928 Pontiac when Dad was driving. This would have been in 1931. My sister Marian would have been five years old, Robert seven, and Wilma Jean nine. They were in the backseat. Soon I was somewhat more mobile and no longer on my mother's lap. I joined my brother and sisters in the backseat.

Our 1928 Pontiac had two separate front seats and a full backseat area. There were only two doors for entry, one on each side. To get into the backseat, you had to fold the back of the front seat forward, then move carefully into the back. The back of that front seat was then moved into its original position.

Normal top speed for that car was around thirty-five mile per hour. Relatively soon, our two-door 1928 Pontiac was replaced by a 1929 four-door Chevrolet. All four Carter children could now enter directly into the backseat, and we would usually travel thirty-five miles an hour on the country dirt roads—maybe a bit faster on paved roads. That was a good speed for country folks in the cars of that era.

This was before seat belts. We just sat quietly and firmly in our seat as we progressed down the road. This was also before air conditioning and heating systems for automobiles.

The first radio I remember was our small battery-operated radio. It was about the size of a shoebox. It was utilized only for news broadcasts once or twice a day. Then in the early 1930s, the *Fibber McGee and Molly* radio show became popular. This was the earliest and most popular public entertainment program available, long before television. Some neighbors did not even have a radio. We would always listen to *Fibber McGee and Molly*. That was the only entertainment program on the radio that I recall Dad or Mom listening to.

Chapter 9

OUR LARGE GARDEN

OUR GARDEN REQUIRED A LOT of work. There is not much garden work that a preschooler can do, but I was learning the process and beginning to help with the simplest part of garden work when my parents were present. My brother, Robert, and sisters Wilma Jean and Marian were also assisting with the duties required in the garden.

When I was five years old, I was spending time on my hands and knees pulling weeds from the growing vegetable rows when my mother or father was close by. Soon I was old enough to use the hoe to chop more weeds down so the vegetables would properly grow. Year by year, I was adding more gardening skills. It would be another two or three years before I was old enough to be of major assistance with the garden work.

In early spring, Dad would plow the garden and complete the soil preparation with the disk and the harrow. Then we could plant lettuce, carrots, beets, peas, potatoes, and other garden items. Our potato patch was quite large. We also had a popcorn and a sweet-corn patch. Virtually every day in the spring, summer, and fall, we spent time in that garden. Mom, Dad, and my brother and sisters did the more difficult hoeing needed. I was still learning garden work by observing what they were doing and participating in the simpler tasks.

The garden was a major source of food for our family. When the vegetables grew to maturity, it was time to begin the canning process. After proper preparation in the kitchen, the vegetables would be placed into pint, quart, or half-gallon glass jars and then carefully sealed and taken to the cellar at the back of our house for storage.

The cellar was never hot in the summer and never cold in the winter. It provided year-round safe storage for the canned food items, and very frequently my mother went down in the cellar to get a pint or quart jar or two of the canned items and bring them to the kitchen to utilize in preparing our three meals a day.

The cellar was constructed by digging down into the ground about ten to twelve feet. Then brick walls were put into place, and the soil from the digging process was placed back on top of the brick roof. This kept the cellar at a moderately cool temperature year-round.

This was in the 1930s, and we did not yet have electricity. We had an icebox. Each week at the local grocery store, Dad would purchase a small block of ice, enough to keep the heavily encased icebox cool for about seven days before the ice melted away. Portions of our daily food supply were kept in the icebox. We had to keep a large pan underneath the icebox for the water from the slowly melting block of ice to drain into.

Chapter 10

RURAL MAIL DELIVERY
IN THE 1930S

F ROM THE NEAREST POST OFFICE, the mailman would drive by automobile out into the country and place the mail in our mailbox—a metal fixture on top of a short post implanted firmly into the ground on the side of the road. When you had letters to mail, you would open the front of the shoebox-size mailbox and put the letters inside. When this was done, you would raise a small metal flag-like device on the mailbox as a message to the mailman that there was outgoing mail to be picked up. If he didn't have any mail to deliver to you, he would not stop unless he saw that device indicating that there was outgoing mail.

To pick up our mail after the mailman had completed his route required a trip to our distant mailbox. At this relatively nearby intersection, there were other mailboxes for those residing on farms off to the right and left. In the winter months in northern Missouri, a major snow day could make the road by our house impassible. If it rained or snowed excessively, the trip would have to be made on horseback or on the tractor.

The trip to our mailbox was about three quarters of a mile from our house and was usually made in our 1928 Pontiac. To keep the roadway in proper travel condition, those living along that road pulled a heavy road drag up and down the road with a team of horses or by tractor. Dad and the other neighborhood farmers would provide the equipment and time required to keep that dirt road in proper passable condition.

Dad also used our horse-drawn mowing machine to trim the weeds growing along the side of our rural road. Several neighborhood farmers performed the same duties along their farm area. Except for heavy rain or major snowstorms, our roadway was reasonably passable. The county seat town of Bethany was a few miles to the southeast. Our nearest small town was Martinsville, and it was just a short distance to the northwest.

When I started second grade, we moved to our second farm. We were now on the daily mail delivery route, and it was just out the door and check the mailbox right in front of our house. We also had daily morning delivery of the St. Joseph, Missouri newspaper. The deliveryman would drive along the roadway early in the morning with each newspaper rolled and tied tightly together. He had a list of subscribers and would know the proper houses where he would toss the rolled newspaper onto the front lawn as he drove by. He never stopped.

For those subscribers living further down a side road, he would toss the newspaper at the nearest intersection where their road reached his daily route. They would have to drive or take a horseback ride to this intersection to pick up their daily newspaper.

Chapter 11

OUR ONE-ROOM
COUNTRY SCHOOL

THERE WERE USUALLY ABOUT TWELVE students in grades one through eight when I started school in 1934 at the Mount Tabor one-room country school. It was located a few miles to the north of Bethany in northwest Missouri. From our farm it was about a half mile walk to the school. Robert, Marian, and I walked to school, as did all others living on farms in the nearby neighborhood. My sister Wilma Jean rode her horse to Martinsville High School a few miles to the northwest.

This was before we could turn a faucet on for daily water needs. It was the duty of the upper-age boys to carry buckets of water every day from the well nearby in the schoolyard. Students had their own individual cup or glass with their name on it for drinking. It would be filled with a dipper from the bucket of water. No one ever drank directly from the dipper or dipped their cup into the bucket of water.

There were two small outhouses in the schoolyard, one for the boys and one for the girls. This was grade school life in rural America in the early 1930s. We had a fifteen-minute recess midmorning and mid afternoon for anyone requiring a trip to the outhouse. At lunchtime, there was an hour break. That provided time for some softball or other simple playground activity.

Every morning my mother would prepare the sandwiches and cookies or a piece of cake for us to take to school for lunch. These items were wrapped in a piece of newspaper or in a small paper container. Before long, we would have a small metal container called a lunch box in which Mom would place our sandwiches for our noon meal.

One winter day at Mount Tabor School a light drizzle began and the temperature dropped quickly below freezing. This resulted in an icy surface on top of the snow. We had a gentle slope down the schoolyard to the country road passing by. It was normally a safe sled ride down that snowy slope.

That day I rushed outside after lunch and was the first to grab my sled. I was having the fastest sled ride of my life down that icy surface. However, at the bottom of the slope I was unable to make the normal safe turn onto the roadway. I shot right on across the road and slammed into a barbed wire fence. That caused a major bleeding gash on my cheek.

Our teacher was Margaret Scott, and she walked to a nearby house and telephoned my mother, advising her that I needed to get to the doctor immediately. This was long before cell phones, and we did not have a telephone in the Mount Tabor country schoolhouse.

Unfortunately, Dad was not at home. Mom had to call our neighbor Alva Groves to come by and pick Mom up then on to the Mount Tabor School for me and we made it reasonably quickly to Doctor Harned's office in Bethany in the Groves Model T Ford. In that relic old car of his we had a safer ride on slick and icy roads than we would have had in his newer automobile.

A scar on my left cheek remained for decades from that accident. Also, it was a major lesson for our schoolteacher that it was best for us not to be riding a sled down a slope where there was a barbed wire fence across the road at the bottom of the hill. No more sled riding at Mount Tabor after that.

Chapter 12

LIFE ON OUR SECOND FARM

IT BECAME EVIDENT THAT WE needed to make a move. We needed to be on a roadway where the high school bus would come right by our house. This prompted my parents to sell our first farm and move to the north of Martinsville where the high school bus route came right by our house.

Wilma Jean was now in her second high school year and would be on the daily school bus ride to Martinsville High School. I was now in second grade and Robert, Marian, and I were attending the Long Branch one-room country school on the corner of this farm. It was only a quarter of a mile walk for us. That was a much quicker walk to school than on our first farm.

A recent photo of the deteriorated Long Branch schoolhouse

I was old enough now to understand more about daily life on the farm. We had both dairy cows and a herd of beef cows. At milking time each evening, the dairy cows were separated from the beef cows out in the pasture and brought to the dairy barn. The dairy cows knew there would be some feed for them in the cow barn, so it was relatively easy to get them moving when I headed out into the pasture in the evening to bring them in at milking time.

We had a collie dog named Queen, and she would be with me. She was very helpful in bringing in the dairy cows. She had a litter of puppies every year. One day after she'd had another litter of puppies, Dad advised me that we had to get rid of Queen. A litter of puppies every year was just too many puppies.

However, he told me I could pick one of the puppies to keep. I made my pick and named him Laddie. I had just read the book *Lad, a Dog* and had been impressed with the story of that young dog in his early days. I would spend much time with that fine puppy when I was doing the simple chores of feeding the chickens and going out into the pasture each evening to separate the dairy cows from the beef cattle. Laddie was always with me. I remember one special day when he was about a year old.

We had a dairy cow that was sometimes stubborn about getting to the barn with the rest of the cows. The cows would be grazing in the pasture along with the beef cattle and had to be properly separated from the dairy cows. This cow wasn't interested.

My father had done nothing to train Laddie about how to be of assistance in driving cattle or horses from the pasture to the barn. As a relatively young dog, he was just tagging along as I separated the dairy cows from the beef cattle each evening and brought them to the barn for milking. Laddie had learned to jump in and gently nip on the back heel of a cow to get her moving whenever needed. One evening, after I had brought the cows in at milking time, I realized that there was one dairy cow missing.

I started slowly up the pasture slope with Laddie at my side, and I tried something different. When I saw this particular dairy cow, I simply motioned toward the area where she was in the midst of the beef cattle and told Laddie to go get her. He obviously had learned the difference in appearance of the dairy cows and the beef cows, and he headed quickly to where she was.

As soon as she saw him coming, she stopped grazing and watched him approach. He arrived and nipped her on her heel, and she got the message. He got her headed for the dairy barn from the midst of the beef cattle in the pasture. That was quite an unusual accomplishment for Laddie and a great farm memory for me.

A few years later as I was growing stronger I could almost keep up with Dad at milking time. Robert was completing other evening chores. Dad and I were doing the hand milking in our small special dairy barn.

Many farm barns at this time had sizable metal pieces providing the roofing. This was a more economical method of roofing a barn than small wood shingles, as were used on farmhouses. This large metal piece was about two to three feet wide and seven to eight feet long. It would produce considerable noise during a winter hailstorm. Our house was shingled with special wooden shingles and therefore not nearly as noisy.

The small hog sheds where the sows were placed when their litter was soon due to be delivered were called the "hog houses" and were scattered about a special lot area near the barn. You could have small one-sow hog sheds or larger two-sow hog sheds depending on the number of sows you owned. My dad was one of the major hog farmers in our neighborhood, and we had several sows. Therefore, we had several hog sheds and a large number of sows and pigs to feed every day.

I was now further into my grade school years and would soon be strong enough to do more of the duties required on our farm. I was helping not only with the morning and evening chores but also with the increasing duties out in the fields year by year..

On our second farm, there was a field where there were many growing trees. We were sawing down trees from this forest area to provide fuel for our wood-burning stoves in the house. The sawing-down process was done with a crosscut saw, which was about five feet in length. Power was provided by one person on each end of the saw bringing it back and forth many times. I was still too young to help Dad or my brother saw down trees but I was observing the process.

First, you had to decide precisely where you wanted the tree to fall. The next part of the procedure was to saw straight into the tree six to eight inches on the side you wanted the tree to fall. Then the saw was removed and placed a few inches above that and angled down to approximately where you sawed into the tree. After sawing out that small tree section, you would remove it.

Next would come the real sawing-down process with the five-foot-long crosscut saw with one person on each end. You would pull that saw back and forth, and soon the tree would fall in the direction of the side-chunk removed at the bottom. When the tree was down, there was more sawing to do. The large and small limbs were sawed into six- to eight-foot logs.

Some of this was done by swinging an axe to trim the smaller branches into very small pieces of wood of proper size for placement in the stove in the kitchen. Our front room heating stove was much different in size and structure. It was required during the cold winter days to provide heating in the house.

The next step was to place the larger tree trunk or tree-limb logs on a proper piece of equipment to hold it firmly in horizontal position. Now it was time to take the five-foot-long crosscut saw, with one of us on each end, and saw the log into pieces of wood about twelve to fourteen inches in length. This required pulling the saw back and forth.

The very large chunks of wood from the tree trunk or large tree-limb area had to be split into smaller pieces. This was done by placing a small piece of sharpened iron about five inches in length properly on the top of this large chunk of wood and pounding on it with a heavy sledgehammer. That would split the chunk of wood into smaller pieces appropriate in size for the wood-burning stoves. The smaller tree limbs were chopped by axe or sawed into small pieces.

Carrying wood from the woodpile to the back porch each evening was one of my early farm duties from the time I started first grade. After we had moved to our second farm, I was strong enough to be doing more farm work with each passing year.

We would soon be purchasing coal to be utilized in the kitchen and heating stoves. This eliminated the need to be sawing down trees. A load of coal would be ordered frequently and emptied into the backyard area where it was handy to be brought as needed to the back porch with a special coal bucket. That bucket would be filled with coal and brought to the back porch for use in both the kitchen and front room stoves. We were now using only a very small quantity of wood, just to get the fire started.

Chapter 13

FAMILY SHOPPING IN THE 1930S AT THE J. C. PENNEY STORE IN BETHANY

THERE WAS A J. C. Penney store in Bethany just a few miles from our farm. This was the most sophisticated store in Bethany at this time in the 1930s. Mr. J. C. Penney was born on his family farm near Hamilton, Missouri, in 1875, a short time before my parents were born. Our farm was just a short distance to the north of Hamilton.

This would have been one of Mr. Penney's very early stores. Now there are more than 1,100 Penney stores nationwide. Mr. Penney lived until 1971. I have driven by his rural home, which was about thirty miles from our farm. It was an ordinary farm similar to the farm area where I was born. My deduction is that he would have been one of the first highly successful entrepreneurs from my home state of Missouri.

At our local J. C. Penney store when I was a youngster in the early 1930s, you selected your items for purchase and took them to a nearby counter. The attendant there entered your purchase and advised you of your total. Then you gave the clerk your payment and it was sent to an office at the back of the store at the open second floor level. This was done by placing the information and payment into a small container attached to an elongated line to the higher open level at the back of the store. Once your money was in that container, the clerk would pull down a short connection that provided the power to send your payment up to the operator.

The operator there would enter all information in his or her piece of equipment, and a receipt and any change due you would be placed in that small container. By gravity, it would come sailing quickly back down to the counter where your purchase was being packaged. That was the clerical purchasing process as done at our J. C. Penney Store in Bethany, Missouri.

In my early years in grade school in the 1930s, my parents allowed me to walk around the Bethany square all by myself while they did the necessary purchasing of items needed for the following week. I would soon move on into a small store on the south side of the square when I did not want any more walking. I would just sit and wait for Dad or Mom to come by and get me when it was time for the drive back home. They knew the precise store where I would be waiting for them.

Chapter 14

PREPARING FARM FIELDS
FOR CROP PLANTING WITH
MACHINERY IN THE 1930S

I N THE MID-1930S, DAD WAS carefully teaching me the duties required
of young boys and early teenagers on the farm. After the early morning
chores of feeding the livestock and chickens were completed, it was time to
harness the horses and get the tractor into operation. I learned all of this
farm operation mostly by being with Dad and observing what he and my
brother were doing.

Robert was helping Dad prepare the cropland for planting in the early
spring before I was old enough to be doing any heavy work. Some farmers
at that time still did not have tractors. Teams of horses were utilized for
fieldwork. My father reportedly purchased the first tractor sold in our area
in the late 1920s. Some of the larger farms would have two teams of horses.
At this time in farm history in the very early 1930s there were relatively
few farmers with tractors. They had just come on the market and not yet
in general use.

In my early grade school years, I was doing more tractor-driving duties
and observing and learning in much greater detail the crop planting and
harvesting process. After the fields had been plowed came the disking
process. I could not yet do the more difficult plowing, but I was now
driving the tractor doing much of the disking. Our disk was about twelve
feet in width, with many small sharp wheel-like devices rotating as it was

pulled through the field. This broke the plowed ground further into a finer surface.

After the disking, our team of horses pulled the harrow up and down through the field. This piece of equipment was about twelve feet wide with many small sharp metal pieces that would complete the process of breaking down the soil surface and making the field ready for planting.

I was still in my preteen years but capable of observing all farm work and driving the team of horses back and forth through the field with Dad in the back of the wagon keeping the rotating planting equipment scooped full of wheat or oats. After the field had been planted, it was time to draw the harrow back and forth through the field. This would gently mix the grain into the soil. Now it was time to wait a few days, and we would soon observe the crop beginning to grow.

Chapter 15

CORN PLANTING AND HARVEST IN THE 1930S

T HE PROCESS OF PLANTING CORN in the early 1930s and on into the 1940s was somewhat more complicated than planting wheat and oats. After the field had been plowed, disked, and harrowed, the planter would be drawn through the field by our team of horses. On the corn planter there were two relatively small containers about three to four feet across from each other into which the seed corn would be placed.

A rotating piece of the planter would drop the seed corn down into the soil as it was pulled back and forth across the cultivated field. The seedlings were gently covered with cultivated soil. It was necessary to have a parked wagon at the side of the field with a supply of seed corn for frequently refilling the small containers on the corn planter.

The cornfield was usually about thirty or forty acres in size on our 160-acre farm. After the corn had grown for a few days, it was time to pull the cultivator up and down through the cornfield with our team of horses. This would keep weeds from overtaking the rows of growing corn. The cultivator had very small plow-like devices, and they would turn the soil gently over between the rows of corn and eradicate the growing weeds. The cornstalks would soon grow to about six feet in height with the ears of corn at about waist level.

When harvest time came, we shucked the corn by hand. As the wagon was pulled through the field by the team of horses I could, in my early preteen years; shuck one row of corn while Dad shucked two. A few years later I was shucking two rows along with Dad. The horses were trained to follow a row of corn with one on each side of a row of already shucked corn.

They were also trained to follow the orders of "get up" and "whoa." No one had to be in the wagon driving the team—except when the end of the row had been reached and it was time to get back in the wagon to get the team of horses properly started back through the field again.

For the corn-shucking procedure, we used a special small device with a hook on it strapped on the right hand. Shucking involved scraping that little hook firmly along the dried husk of ripened corn. Then you could with your own hands break that open ear of corn from the cornstalk and toss it into the wagon.

The wagon had a special high board area along the opposite side, and you would firmly and quickly toss the shucked ears of corn against it. That would bounce the ear of corn down into the wagon. When the wagon was full of shucked corn, it was pulled to the corncrib by the team of horses. With a scoop shovel, the load of corn was unloaded into the crib. Several loads of corn could be harvested per day.

When I was twelve years old, I worked about ten hours a day in the cornfields during the summer months. This was corn harvesting for us in the 1930s and into the 1940s. More modern equipment is available today.

Each evening, when it was time to feed the livestock it was necessary to shell the grains of corn off the cob. This was done with our small corn sheller. By turning the corn sheller crank around and around up and down, and feeding the open ears of corn into the top of the system, out the bottom into a bucket would come the shelled corn. The bare cobs came out of the sheller end, producing a pile of corncobs. In the cold winter months those cobs were utilized in our kitchen and front room stoves. They were especially important in the early part of starting the fire.

Chapter 16

PLANTING AND HARVESTING OUR WHEAT AND OAT CROPS

W HEN I REACHED MY EARLY teen years in the early 1940s, I became much more involved with farm work. I was now out in the fields helping with the sowing of wheat and oats. We had a special wagon with a mechanical device at the back. When this wagon containing the wheat or oats for planting was pulled through the properly prepared field, one person would drive the team of horses or the tractor and another would be in the back area of the wagon. With a scoop shovel, the person in back would keep the grain scooped into a large funnel part of the equipment.

This small piece of planting equipment was motor-driven and a horizontal rotating part would send the grains of wheat or oats out the back of the wagon, providing a twelve-to fifteen-foot-wide planted area behind the wagon. Dad was the operator of this equipment. My brother or I would be driving the tractor-pulled wagon back and forth across the field, and Dad would keep the container part of the equipment properly scooped full of wheat or oat seeds. With that complete, next came the horse-drawn harrow back and forth across the field. This provided the appropriate soil covering for the scattered seeds of wheat or oats.

When the crops were grown to proper maturity it was time for harvest. This started with our grain binder, which was pulled and powered by the tractor. It had an elongated mowing section onto which the mowed stems of wheat or oats would feed. This had a constantly rotating canvas that was feeding those stems of mowed wheat or oats into and through the system. Then out of the high back part of the grain binder would come many bundles of wheat or oats tied together with small strips of binder twine.

One was driving the tractor pulling the grain binder and another sitting on a high seat at the back of the binder operating that piece of equipment. As a young teenager, I would be driving the tractor pulling the binder and Dad would be sitting on that special seat doing the professional binder operation. The now tied-together bundles of wheat or oats were scattered all across the field and had to be shocked.

Eight or ten bundles were placed together by placing the straw part on the ground, and building a shock. Row upon row of shocked wheat or oats could be seen throughout the field. After a few days of further drying time the threshing machine would be brought to the farm. This very large piece of equipment would be placed in the approximate center of the wheat or oat field.

Now came the threshing process. There was a rotating belt system connecting the power of the stationary full-speed running tractor to the huge stationary threshing machine. In our neighborhood, George Eckard was the operator of this piece of equipment. The threshing machine would be drawn by tractor from farm to farm to complete the wheat and oat harvesting.

About eight horse-drawn hayracks were required to bring the bundles of wheat or oats to the stationary threshing machine. Several neighborhood farmers worked together to complete the wheat or oat harvest, farm by farm. It is now possible to go online and find images of the huge threshing machines of that era.

Filling the hayrack with the bundles was a two-person operation. The hayrack would be drawn through the field by a team of horses and stopped by a shock and one on the ground with a pitchfork would toss the bundles up into the hayrack one bundle at a time. The one in the hayrack would arrange the bundles properly so a maximum load could be gathered. Then this load of wheat or oat bundles would be hauled to the large stationary threshing machine.

The simplest job in this process was to be the one on the ground with a pitchfork pitching the bundles up into the hayracks and that was my first duty at threshing time. The one in the hayrack would properly arrange the bundles so a proper hayrack load could be hauled to the threshing machine.

When tossed by pitchfork into the rotating threshing system, the bundles would be rolled into the interior of the huge thresher, and the wheat or oat grains would be separated from the straw. Out one large long system would come the straw and a major straw stack would begin to form. The grain would feed into another smaller system and would flow constantly and gently into a grain wagon parked beside the thresher.

When that wagon was properly filled, it would be pulled by a horse-team to the nearby grain bin, and with a scoop shovel was emptied into the bin. A second wagon was now receiving the grain flowing out of the thresher. Depending on the number of acres of grain to be harvested it usually took two or three days of threshing time to complete the process for each farm.

Several neighborhood housewives working together in the kitchen and dining room prepared and served the noon meal for this large hardworking crew of fourteen to fifteen men and teenage boys who would come in from the field hungry and ready for plenty of food at lunchtime.

Soon came a new piece of equipment that made the huge threshing machine history. This was the combine. At proper harvest time it was pulled through the field of growing wheat or oats by a tractor. The grain was immediately separated from the straw and fed into a grain wagon. The straw remained strewn over the field from the combine. There would be many loads of grain to be hauled and scooped into the grain bin with the scoop shovel.

We would sometimes use the sulky rake out in the field to build rows of straw and a small straw stack or two. Some of this straw would be hauled to the barn for storage. It was utilized in the horse stalls or dairy barn. Any straw remaining about the field would simply be turned underground by the plow when it came time to prepare the field for planting again.

Chapter 17

OUR HAY CROPS

HAVING A BARN LOFT FULL of hay was a necessity for the cattle and horses. This consisted primarily of alfalfa and clover. Out in the field after the soil was properly prepared for planting, the hayseed would be placed into a piece of equipment in the back of a wagon. It was pulled through the field by a team of horses or the farm tractor. With a small motor-driven circulation, the hayseed would be scattered over the top of the properly prepared soil as the wagon was pulled back and forth.

One person drove the team of horses or tractor pulling the wagon while another kept the hayseeds scooped into the equipment. After this phase was completed, the horse-drawn harrow would be pulled back and forth through the field, gently rolling just enough of the tilled soil on top of the crop seeds so they would be ready to begin growth.

When the alfalfa or clover crop had grown to proper maturity, it was mowed with our horse-drawn mowing machine. The next procedure was to rake the hay into long rows with a special sulky rake. After a bit of the mowed hay had been accumulated in the rake, you would step on a little clutch-like device and push it down. That would cause the twelve-foot-wide rake portion to rise and eventually leave a long row of raked hay on the ground.

This procedure continued back and forth across the field, leaving many rows of raked hay. Then it was time to build a haystack. This required a bull rake. My first job out in the hayfield was driving the team of horses hitched to this rake. This rake had many long wooden pieces just a few inches apart and approximately ten feet in length straight across the front of the ten-foot-wide rake on the ground.

There was a horse hitched on each side of the twelve-foot rake. My first duty in the hayfield was to drive the team of horses bringing this load of hay to the side of the developing haystack. This was nothing like driving a team of horses side by side pulling a wagon. At the side of the haystack, the team would be backed up, leaving the load of hay on the ground beside the developing stack

My brother would pitch this hay up onto the haystack with his pitchfork. Meanwhile, Dad was on top of the growing stack with his pitchfork, properly spreading the hay around. This required constantly walking around to get the hay firmly and properly in place. The stacking procedure required far more skill than driving a bull rake or pitching hay.

When the height of the stack reached an eight to ten-foot level, a hay wagon would be horse-drawn through the field and loaded from the raked rows of hay. Then that hayrack load of hay was pulled to the stack and tossed by pitchfork up to a higher level onto the developing haystack.

Soon came a more modern piece of equipment to make the hay harvest more efficient. It would be placed beside the haystack. This was called the hay stacker. Power to operate it was provided by one horse hitched to the device. When a bull-rake load of hay was emptied onto that system, that one horse would be led forward providing the rotating power to lift the load of hay up and dump it on top of the developing stack.

This was the simplest part of the procedure, and therefore it was my first job in the hayfield when I was seven to ten years old. I would lead the horse forward and then back him up into original position. After the load of hay had been lifted up and dumped onto the stack, Dad would scatter the hay about to properly build the developing haystack. My brother would then drive the horse team on the bull rake back into the field for another load of hay.

Before long, I was old enough to be driving the team of horses bringing the bull-rake load of hay to the stack and then taking a few minutes to quickly lead the single horse forward, providing the power to dump that load of hay up on top of the stack. At this point in time, both Dad and Robert were usually on top of the much larger stack, quickly taking care of the stacking process.

This made hay harvest and stacking more efficient than the former process of pitching hay by pitchfork up from ground level to the top of the developing haystack. A much larger stack of hay could now be created. Relatively soon, I was learning the hay stacking process myself and was joining Dad on top of the stack. Robert was taking care of the on-the-ground duties. After I had helped Dad with the stacking a few times, I was assigned one day to be on top of the haystack all by myself. I was twelve years old.

That would result in my first major lesson in stacking hay. After I had topped off that stack, it looked fine. However, a few days later the stack had settled and was leaning to one side almost like it was going to fall over. I realized then that I had not walked constantly over the top of the stack, firming the hay carefully and properly. Dad was never critical of that improper stack of hay. He was gently teaching me how to spread the hay all over the top of the stack and then to firm it in place by constantly walking over it.

When it came time to haul some hay to the barn hayloft, a hayrack would be drawn along beside the haystack by the team of horses and filled with hay. There was a small outside door on the barn up at hayloft level. Through that opening one would pitch the loose hay from the hayrack into the hayloft by pitchfork. Another inside the loft would scatter the hay about properly. The alfalfa or clover hay was fed daily to the horses, cows, or sheep. It was far better nourishment than grass growing in the pasture.

In the 1940s would come our brand-new hay baler. It was pulled by tractor through the field of mowed hay after the hay was raked into rows by the sulky rake. There was a small motor on the baler feeding the hay into the baling system, and soon there would be a large, very firmly packed bale of hay secured with baling wire.

That bale would be dropped to the ground and another bale immediately started. The growing number of bales would then be stacked out in the field or hauled to the barn hayloft. Stacking a large number of bales in the barn or out in the field and covering them with a large piece of canvas made hay harvest far more efficient than the former process of stacking freshly mowed hay. This was taking place in my later high school and then college years.

Now Robert would be driving the tractor pulling the hay baler, and Dad and I would be perched on a seating device on either side of the baler, placing a tool in proper place at the proper time and then inserting the baling wire so bale after bale of hay would be properly created. That further simplified hay harvest.

The bales of hay strewn throughout the field were hauled to the barn with our hayrack and then tossed into the hayloft. Once in the loft, the bales would be stacked carefully together to get a maximum number of bales into the loft. When the loft was full, the remainder of the bales would be stacked quickly out in the field with a large piece of canvas secured firmly across the top so the hay would not be soaked with rainwater.

Stacking bales of hay was far more efficient than stacking loose hay. When hay was needed for the livestock, a bale of hay would be opened by cutting the baling wire with a special small device and scattering the hay about into a special feeding system.

I was not yet old enough to do absolutely all that Dad and my brother were doing, but it was enough that Robert was now able to spend time working for neighbors. This income built his bank account to provide the funds for his college education. This was back in the 1940s. I have not worked on a farm since graduating from college in 1950 and therefore I am not personally totally familiar with modern farm equipment and farming operations of today.

Chapter 18

MORE DETAILS ON MY EARLY FARM LIFE

F ROM THE GRAIN BIN, WHEAT, oats, or corn would be run through our feed grinder. It was a relatively small piece of equipment that was powered by a belting system from the stationary tractor. That produced powdery grain to be placed in small quantities in the feed trough from which the livestock could eat.

For the hogs, the powdered grain was placed into a barrel of water. This was all stirred and mixed together with the water and some special minerals purchased at a local store to be fed to the hogs at ground level. This procedure was called slopping the hogs.

Our farm horses had individual feed boxes in the barn, and they were brought in from the pasture six days a week. They would always go to their own individual stalls, and we would put a halter on the horses and secure them. For the dairy cows, there was a special part of the dairy barn with a row of stanchions for securing the cows when evening milking time arrived.

We placed the feed for the dairy cows properly along the row of stanchions, and then the barn door would be opened and the dairy cows would immediately come in from the lot. I cannot explain this, but they would somehow go right to their own special stalls. It didn't make any difference to us which stall they were in, but it seemed that each cow knew the precise stall where she would go every evening. There was always special feed for the cows in their stalls.

Dad always had a sizable number of hog sheds scattered throughout the barn lot area. The sows would be confined when they were near the time to deliver their litter of pigs. After a few more weeks, the pigs were separated from their mother sow and placed in a pen adjoining the barn lot.

They would be fed and watered every day. There were usually eight to ten little pigs per litter. Water for the pigs and sows was carried in buckets to a ground-level water trough. For the chickens or turkeys, there was a special container to be filled with water that would flow as needed to a lower level.

For the livestock water supply on our first firm, we had a cistern near the barn—a well with a water pump. There was a special piping system along the lower edges of the large barn roof sending the water properly into the well during rainstorms. This is why it was called a cistern. The water was not coming from a natural underground source on this farm. It was rainwater carefully piped into the nearby cistern from the very large barn roof.

Horses and cattle drank directly from the large water tank by the barn or the one out in the field that was filled by a wind-powered pumping system—a windmill. The pigs, small young calves, and chickens had to receive their water from a ground-level trough system. That required carrying water bucketful by bucketful and emptying the buckets into the watering trough. This was part of the morning and evening farm chores.

If there were an excess number of days without rainfall, we would have to haul water from the windmill tank out into the pasture and empty it into this well by the barn. That was done with a special large water tank that was kept permanently in one of our wagons. It was far too large to be removed and then reloaded periodically.

We would pull this wagon with a shortened tongue by the tractor to the windmill water tank out in the pasture. That was all this wagon was used for. We had other wagons for other farm needs. Filling this tank was done bucketful by bucketful from the water tank beside the windmill.

When the tank in the wagon was full, it was pulled back to the barn lot and emptied into the cistern there. This was done by backing the wagon to the cistern and then removing a very large bolt-like device at the bottom end of the elongated tank. That devise was fastened permanently by chain to the bottom end of the tank. As soon as that small device was removed, water from the tank would flow forcefully into the cistern.

It usually required at least two tanks of water to properly fill the cistern if there had been little to no rain for several days. This was our water supply for the livestock in pens around the barn lot on our first farm. If we had sufficient periodic rain, the rainwater flowing off the barn roof and piped into the nearby well would normally provide sufficient water for this location.

From the well by the barn, we would pump up buckets of water to carry to the hog lot or chicken house each day. This was one of my early farm chores, even when I could only carry a gallon bucket full of feed or water. We had another well near the back door of our first farm home for water needs in the kitchen.

Later at our second farm we did not have a well near the house. Water supply at this house was taken care of by placing two large five- or ten-gallon cream-can containers in the backseat of our car and filling them at a distant well. They were then brought to the kitchen. Water was dipped out of the large container into a bucket placed on a small shelf area where it was available for daily water needs in the house.

The chickens were fed and watered every day, and this was one of my first farm duties as soon as I was twelve years old on our second farm. I would carry buckets of water to the chicken house from a nearby well. We also had a small shed near the chicken house with the proper daily supply of feed. After feeding and watering the hens I would gather the eggs into a bucket each evening and take them to the nearby shed where we had a large egg case. One by one, the eggs were carefully placed into the egg case for storage.

Once each week the case full of eggs and a large five or ten-gallon can of cream would be taken to a nearby store and sold. This would provide all income necessary to cover the cost of grocery items needed in the kitchen plus a few dollars for the family bank account.

Chapter 19

OUR SECOND FARM

OUR SECOND FARM WAS LOCATED on a graveled road that was maintained regularly for travel regardless of weather. It was located just a few miles to the north of Martinsville in northwest Missouri. The electrical lines were being installed on tall sturdy poles beside the road. A proper connection was made to houses along the roadway. We now had electricity in the house. It was not as complete as electricity we enjoy today but for us it was a major change in farm life.

My dad was a part of the crew that installed the large tall poles on which the electrical lines were installed along the roadway by our house. There were still many rural roadways where electric lines were not available.

We could now flip a switch and have a light on in the front room, dining room or kitchen. Hand-carried kerosene-powered lamps were still required in the bedrooms. Our icebox was now history and we had a refrigerator. Our heating system continued to be wood-burning or coal-burning stoves. Our underground cellar just to the back of the house was still needed to hold the large supply of canned food items from the garden. Our radio was still battery operated. This was before television.

During my early teenage years I was occasionally working for other nearby farmers making a dollar or two a day. One of my notable early farm memories involved helping a neighbor fill his silo. We did not have a silo on our farm, so this was a new experience for me. This silo was a very tall round concrete structure about twelve feet in diameter and built to a height of about eighty feet. There were silos on other farms, but some were not nearly as tall.

The silo would be filled with ground sorghum stalks. Sorghum growing in the field looks somewhat like corn, but there are no ears. The growing stalks have different nutritional benefits for livestock. At harvest time, the sorghum stalks growing in the field would be mowed down and hauled to the silo. There the stalks would be pitched into a piece of equipment powered by a belt system with a nearby stationary tractor. This piece of equipment would chop the sorghum stalks into small bits.

The chopped sorghum was called silage, and it would feed into a large vertical piping system that would send it up and into the tall round silo beside the barn. This would eventually fill the silo from ground level far up to the top. Someone with a special wide pitchfork would be strolling around inside the silo spreading the silage carefully around and walking about as the silo was being filled. Thus a maximum amount of silage could be placed in the silo. One day I was assigned to do the silage spreading and firming process on a nearby neighbor's farm all by myself.

Dad and other neighborhood farmers were providing the crew to haul the loads of sorghum stalks to this major piece of equipment. One could enter the silo by way of a permanent vertical ladder system just outside the upright circular wall with small openings from bottom to top. As it was being filled, many small coverings would be placed along the outside of this tall round silo. Thus there was a special vertical ladder system on the outside of the silo.

When the silo had been filled to top level, the way to exit was to crawl slowly and carefully out over the top of that very tall structure and get my feet on the permanent vertical ladder system along the outside of the silo. This was the first time I had ever been at this height looking straight down to ground level. Crawling out over the top of the silo was a breathtaking experience. I got my feet safely onto the permanent ladder system and slowly completed my safe exit straight down the outside ladder to ground level.

That remains a very vivid farm-life memory for me. One small error could have resulted in a major fall and a serious life-threatening injury. Adult farmers were accustomed to this particular farm duty, but it was the first time for me.

I received a ten-dollar bill as payment for my time assisting with the filling of that silo. To me, that was a sizable sum of money. My occasional continuing income from working for neighbors was going into my own bank account in nearby Bethany. No check was written until I started college.

Chapter 20

RURAL TELEPHONE SERVICE IN THE 1930S AND 1940S

I N THE EARLY 1930S TELEPHONE lines were strewn along roadways out in the country. Telephone poles were large and steady and approximately twenty to thirty feet in height. Those crossing a road had to be taller than the ones along the roadside. This was because trucks were frequently hauling products to or from a farm that was located on one of those country roadways.

Most rural homes had a telephone on the wall in the center of the house so it would be handy to make a call or answer a call if you heard your ring. The telephone itself was a wooden boxlike piece of equipment. There could be others on your line and when you heard your ring you went to the telephone, took the receiver off the hook on the upper side, and said hello into a special open piece on the front side of that sizable telephone.

Our ring on the second farm was a long and a short and a long. Other nearby neighbors on our line would have different combinations of long and short rings. Therefore, when you heard the telephone ringing, you had to listen carefully to see if it was for you.

The receiver device was on the upper left side of the telephone. To make a call you would take the small receiver off the hook and listen to be sure there was no one in conversation on your line. There would be a few neighbors on your line, so you had to be very careful when you were ready to make a telephone call.

To make a call to a nearby neighbor who was also on your line, you would take the receiver off the hook to be sure your line was clear and then turn a little crank on the right side of the telephone around and around. That would send the ring down the telephone line to your neighbor's telephone.

You could hear the rings of nearby neighbors who were also on your line—and they could listen in on any telephone conversation you might be having. If you were making a distant call, you had to call telephone central in nearby Martinsville. There was an operator on duty twenty-four hours a day. When you called central the operator would answer your call, and you would tell him or her who you were calling and the town or city where they lived. The operator would connect you to that central office, and the operator there would complete your call.

How far we have come when we can now pick up our little cell phone and immediately complete a telephone call to anyone living thousands of miles away. For those of us on the farm in the 1930s and 1940s there was sometimes a long wait just to be sure your local neighborhood telephone line was not busy. That was telephone service at its best when I was a youngster on the farm in the 1930s and early 1940s.

Chapter 21

A RIDE IN MY GRANDFATHER CARTER'S MODEL T FORD

My Carter grandparents, Adam and Frances Carter, lived on a farm a few miles to the south of ours. We would drive to their house one Sunday a month. Their garage was a double-car garage, and they had kept their very first Model T Ford. We did not have a garage on our farm. Henry Ford had built the first Model T in 1893. That was just a few years before my parents were born in 1896.

That provides for me another quick visualization of what life was like for my father and mother when they were youngsters in the early 1900s. Dad was a farm boy and Mom was a small-town girl.

I had never seen the old Model T outside his garage until one day when Grandfather Carter drove it the relatively short distance to our farm. This was in 1936 when I was seven years old and this would be my second and last ride in a Model T. He must have had a pretty knowledgeable mechanic to help him keep that car in operable condition. It would have been one of the first cars manufactured by Henry Ford.

Grandfather Carter never drove that old car on a regular basis. He had a fine new automobile for everyday use. This particular day, Dad was not home. He was off helping one of our neighbors so Grandfather Carter asked if I would like to take a ride in his relic old car. Naturally I said yes. I was still only about eight years old.

When we were but a short distance down the road the car sputtered and the engine stopped running. We were just sitting there. Grandpa asked if I thought I could get it cranked and started for him again. He had to be inside ready to manipulate the little lever just below the steering wheel while someone else was out in front doing the hand cranking. I could tell he was seriously concerned.

I had helped Dad get our tractor cranked and going a few times so I was familiar with the procedure. I was successful in my first and only experience of car cranking. He was very quickly on his way home. That was my last ride in a Model T Ford.

Chapter 22

THE MUSICAL TALENT OF
MY MOTHER'S FAMILY

M Y GRANDFATHER COVER ON MY mother's side of the family was employed with a weekly newspaper in Bethany, Missouri but would soon move short distance to the nearby small growing town of New Hampton. There he opened a printing shop and established his own weekly newspaper. This was the *New Hampton Tribune*. That was a successful venture for him. He had to get out and sell the advertising and then get back to the printing shop and complete the publishing of his weekly newspaper.

His son Rodney, my mother's youngest brother, was working for him at this time operating the linotype and being of major assistance in the publication of this small-town weekly newspaper. Except for my mother and Rodney, the other sons and daughters were living in the Kansas City area. Rodney would soon also move on to Kansas City and become a member of one of the popular Kansas City Bands.

It was well known by nearby neighbors and friends in New Hampton that a Sunday afternoon Cover family gathering would include a professional musical performance. This could involve any or all of the Cover sons and daughters and their families—Albert, Frank, Don, Fred, Rodney, Norma, and my mother Leah.

When neighbors observed that there was this kind of summertime family gathering under way they would bring their own chairs or blankets to spread across the front lawn in the early afternoon. They knew there would be a fine musical performance right there in their own neighborhood. The front lawn would soon be full.

My Uncle Rodney with his professional musical experience in Kansas City would usually start the Sunday Afternoon family entertainment sitting at the piano playing many of the songs he knew. He didn't have to carry music with him. All he needed was a list of song titles. Soon his brothers and sisters would gather around and sing in perfect harmony many of the songs they all knew. It was in perfect harmony.

It was truly an afternoon of fine musical entertainment. There was bass, baritone, and tenor for the men and alto and soprano for the women. Don Cover could not only sing, but he was also a performing solo dancer.

One summer Sunday we were enjoying dinner at my sister Wilma Jean's house. The front room was crowded. Many family members were present and all the chairs were taken. I was sitting with Uncle Rodney on the piano bench as we looked back across the front room. This was when I was a freshman at the University of Missouri and was singing just for fun with other musically inclined friends. With them I had learned the country song "Mountain Dew." On this occasion, I asked Rodney if he knew it.

His answer was "No, I don't think I have ever heard that song. How does it go?"

I sang it through for him as he turned to face the piano and started pecking away on the keyboard. We went through it twice, slowly and carefully. Then he turned to me and said, "Okay, I've got it. Let's go." I started singing "Mountain Dew" again, and he was all over that piano from top to bottom with both hands. He was not chording. It was as if he had been playing that song all his life.

The Cover family knew dozens of songs. At our first farmhouse in the country, we had an open stairway leading from the front room up to the second floor. On occasion we would have a Sunday gathering of the Cover family there. My mother's brother Don would always take advantage of the opportunity to not only harmonize with his brothers and sisters but also tap dance up and down that open stairway and into the front room and adjoining dining room for the benefit of all present.

Rodney's daytime job was in the printing profession. He was talented and speedy on the linotype. He was often busy during the evening playing piano with a local band. If he was free any night without a band performance, he was usually playing piano for an evening of live musical entertainment at a fine Kansas City restaurant.

In addition to our Cover family gatherings, one Sunday each month we would go to my grandfather and grandmother Carter's house just north of New Hampton. There would usually be other Carter family members there. It was a friendly noontime meal, sitting and visiting with cousins, aunts, and uncles in their nice country home. Their house remains in fine condition today. However, it has been moved in recent years to a site in nearby Bethany where my sister Wilma Jean's daughter Nancy and her husband Elvis Allen live.

Chapter 23

THE AMISH
NEIGHBORHOOD NEAR
OUR FIRST FARM

WHEN WE WOULD MAKE OUR weekly trip to Bethany from our first farm in northwest Missouri in our 1928 Pontiac we would pass through a neighborhood where we would usually meet neighbors traveling by horse and buggy. This is a memory of mine from when I was still in first grade at the nearby Mount Tabor country school.

On a recent trip through that neighborhood I was reminded that the Amish remain in this community. We were driving along the roadway that had been utilized regularly by my parents for their weekly trip to Bethany from our first farm. We slowed down quickly and carefully when we came up behind a horse-drawn buggy passing through the Amish neighborhood.

Soon the buggy was off the road and heading for home. This was a reminder of what I consider a unique and important part of United States history. A number of Amish families live just to the northwest of Bethany, Missouri. One-room schools have been built to educate Amish children. Families are large, often as many as fifteen children per family. Through the decades once abandoned farms are now filled with dairy cows, chickens, hogs and clothes hanging on the line to dry.

That description is the current mode of living for Amish families. Theirs is a quiet, peaceful, and successful rural neighborhood. For me, this is an important part of the history of my home neighborhood in northwest Missouri.

Chapter 24

MY EARLY INTRODUCTION INTO THE JOURNALISM PROFESSION

M Y GRANDFATHER ON MY MOTHER'S side of the family was J. W. Cover, who published the weekly *New Hampton Tribune* there in New Hampton, Missouri. He had a print shop just to the north of the east-west main street. His printing equipment when I was a youngster in the 1930s was the linotype.

There was a keyboard on the linotype equipment on which the operator would copy handwritten or typed news items. It would come out of the linotype in newspaper form. Some of the large headlines or advertising copy would be handset.

When this was done, the weekly *New Hampton Tribune* was ready for production and then distribution to residents in town and out in the nearby rural neighborhoods. Grandfather Cover's youngest son Rodney provided essential production service on the linotype.

In my early grade school years, we would often visit my mother's family in New Hampton. This was but a short drive from our farm. I would spend time with Grandfather Cover in his printing shop. It was there that I learned how to do the hand setting of individual alphabet letters for some of the advertisements that would appear in the *New Hampton Tribune*. I was also observing the entire publishing procedure of this country-town newspaper.

When the news and advertising copy had been edited together, it was ready for the printing press. I was barely old enough to know how to spell my own name when Grandfather Cover taught me how to hand set it. He helped me print it off on a slip of paper, and I saved that slip of paper for many years.

As printing and publishing equipment became more modernized, the *New Hampton Tribune* became history. The nearby Bethany and Albany newspapers expanded their distribution. Grandfather Cover closed the shop and entered retirement. This was in the 1900s. That resulted in young Rodney Cover moving to Kansas City. He continued in the publishing profession and was also the piano player for one of the popular bands in that large city.

Another memory of note for me in New Hampton was the daily train traveling through downtown just to the north of the east-west main street. There was a grain elevator on the east side of town. Local farmers who had grain from the farm to sell could bring it to this storage facility in New Hampton, and the staff on duty would oversee the transfer of that truckload of grain into the grain elevator. This was in the 1930s and provided income for many area farmers.

Once a week, when the train passed through town, the growing quantity of grain in the large elevator would be transferred to a railway car, and it was off to St. Joseph or Kansas City for further sale and processing. Also, some could be sold to local area farmers needing more grain than they had grown on their own farms.

Today that grain elevator is no longer there and neither is the railway line. The small building that was Grandfather Cover's printing shop still stands, but now it is a small retail shop. There is no newspaper published in New Hampton now. Times have changed in America since the 1930s. Now we can go to our computers and immediately print off our own business cards and research all kinds of information. This was not even dreamed of in the 1930s and early 1940s.

Chapter 25

MORE ABOUT MY
EARLY FARM LIFE

B Y THE TIME I WAS five years old I could drive our harnessed team of
horses in the most simple farm duties. I could simply pull the long
line connection to the horse bridles gently and that would guide the team
to turn to the right or to the left. The verbal commands were "get up" and
"whoa." A turn to the right was "gee" and a turn to the left was "haw."

Then at age twelve years I was ready to help Dad with all farm work.
Getting the tractor motor started required a hand-cranking procedure.
The crank was on the lower front of that sizable tractor. It had to be turned
around and around a few times to get the tractor motor started. This was
well before there were "starters" for farm tractors.

Household duties for my mother and sisters Wilma Jean and Marian
included washing the dishes. This was done by hand in a large dishpan
with a considerable amount of hot water. There was also some powdered
soap to place in the dishpan. The dishes, pots, pans, and silverware would
be properly washed and then placed in another large bowl just to the side.
The teakettle would be utilized to pour hot water over the washed dishes.

They were now rinsed and ready for the drying process. This was done
by hand with a tea towel. After this the dishes, pots, and pans were properly
stacked on kitchen shelves. This was daily kitchen work well before the
modern equipment we have today.

Weeds and grass on our lawn in the 1930s required regular mowing.
This was done with the large mowing machine drawn by our team of

horses. A few years later on the second farm we had a lawn mower. Taking care of the hand-pushed lawn mower soon became one of my early duties on this farm. The turning wheels provided power for the circulating system that would cut the grass. Soon would come the more modern motor-powered lawn mower.

For household use on our first farm there was a well near the back of the house with a hand-powered pump. Every day we had to carry sufficient water to the house for use in the kitchen and for our household drinking-water supply. I was at first doing this with only a gallon bucket while Dad or Robert would carry two large buckets of water in for household use. Later, on our second farm we would carry water from a more distant well or place a five or ten-gallon container in the car and haul it to the house.

For watering the cattle and horses out in the pasture there was a windmill. This was a metallic structure ranging from twenty to thirty feet in height. At the top was a relatively small vertical wheel-like device properly constructed to be whirled around and around by the blowing wind.

This was connected to the pump at ground level by a long rod structure. When turned on, the whirling wind motion at the top would create a very fast up and down movement of that vertical long rod system that would operate the pump and fill the large water tank, providing water for the cattle and horses.

When the water tank was full, the windmill was turned off with a braking system. The pump could then be disconnected from the connection to the top of the windmill and pumped by hand to fill buckets of fresh water needed in the house. Water for the pigs and poultry was dipped from the large water tank and carried by three-gallon buckets to smaller watering systems.

On our first farm, there was also a water tank by the barn that was filled by a system that would feed the rainwater flowing from the roof of the barn into the water tank. When that tank was filled, the water would be directed into the very nearby cistern. From this cistern we would personally pump water as needed for the pigs, chickens, or other livestock that were not tall enough to drink from a three-foot-high water tank.

If we had an excess number of days without rainwater flowing from the barn roof into this well by the barn, we had a sizable tank that was permanently placed in one of our wagons. This tank would be filled bucketful by bucketful from our windmill some distance away and pulled by tractor to that water tank in the barn lot and emptied.

On that first farm there was also a well near the back door of the house for household use. This was when I was in first grade and only involved in the very simplest farm duties. I was walking the approximate three quarters of a mile to our nearby Mount Tabor country school along with Robert and Marian.

My oldest sister Wilma Jean was in her freshman year at Martinsville High School at the time. It would have required a very lengthy walk for her to reach the roadway where the school bus would be passing, so Dad purchased a fine saddle mare for her to make her five-day-a-week ride to high school. That fine young mare's name was Toots. Soon she would have a colt and Dad gave her the name Beauty. Heavy work on the farm was done with our tractor.

We always had two "work horses" to be harnessed six days a week. At first this was Ball and Jim, our large heavy farm team. Later it was just Toots and Beauty when we had a rubber tired tractor which was much more efficient than the older steel wheeled tractor. Toots and Beauty were harnessed six days a week and utilized for pulling smaller equipment about the farm as needed.

During Wilma Jean's first year of horseback riding to high school it became evident that we had to make a move to a farm location where the school bus would be driving right by our house. Soon to follow would be Robert and then Marian and myself. Therefore, that farm was sold and we moved a relatively short distance to a location where the school bus would be driving right by our house.

This was four miles to the north of Martinsville. On that farm household water had to be carried from a more distant well to the house. One of my daily duties on this farm was to assist in carrying small buckets of water to the house when Dad was carrying two large buckets. As the years passed and I grew stronger, I could carry the larger buckets of water when assisting Dad and Robert in all farm chores.

We never had a faucet-supplied teakettle on the kitchen stove. Often a larger container would be filled with water and placed on top of this large rectangular wood-fueled kitchen stove to be heated for bathing and other household use. A considerable amount of water had to be carried daily to the house in buckets. Relatively soon, Dad was hauling water to the house in five-gallon containers placed in a wagon or in the backseat of our automobile.

In addition to the wood-fueled stove in the kitchen we also had a kerosene-fueled kitchen stove with five separate burners. There was a small container of kerosene at one end of this stove, and when a burner was turned on the kerosene would feed into the system and soak up onto the burner. Lighting a match and placing it just above the burner would produce a small safe circular flame providing the heating system for food preparation. There was also an oven for baking purposes.

The first washing machine that I specifically remember was powered by hand with a small upright rod at the side of the washer. This would have been in the 1930s. That rod would be constantly hand-moved back and forth, providing the power to rotate the mechanism inside the washing machine. When that was completed the clothing items were moved through another device called a wringer.

The power for that small device was provided by a cranking system that was hand operated. The water from that procedure would run into an open bucket. The damp clothing items were taken to the clothesline and secured there with clothespins for sunshine and breeze to complete the drying process.

The clothesline consisted of two poles about thirty feet apart. On the top end of the approximately five-foot-tall poles was fastened a special small horizontal board system on which the two lines were attached. After the washing procedure, Wilma Jean and Marian would complete the procedure for pinning the freshly washed clothes along the clothesline. It was a relatively quick process if the sun was shining. If it was raining it was necessary to wait until the rain stopped before placing the washed items on the line to dry. There were other challenges in the cold winter months.

When warm or hot water was needed in the kitchen for hand-washing or dish-washing, a small amount would be poured from the heated teakettle into the dishpan for the dishes or to a wash pan in the sink for hand-washing. For bathing, we would take a sizable pan of warm water to the bedroom and close the door to complete the bathing procedure. At this time in the 1930s and early 1940s, we did not have a bathtub or inside bathroom on our farm.

Chapter 26

LIFE FOR ME ON OUR
SECOND FARM

A FTER WE MOVED TO OUR second farm in 1936 the Martinsville school bus route ran right by our house. The graveled road was well maintained year-round. I was now in second grade at the nearby Long Branch one-room country school and observing many more details about daily farm life in the mid 1930s. Robert, Marian, and I had a much quicker walk to school now than on the first farm. No more horse back riding to high school for any of us. It was just out the front door and a few steps to wait for the school bus.

Three years later Wilma Jean would graduate from Martinsville High School and obtain a job in nearby Bethany. While living there she would meet Dean Murray and they would marry. They purchased a sizable farm a few miles from where we lived and Dean became a very successful farmer. They would have four children, David, Ronald, Nancy, and Joyce.

Next my brother, Robert would graduate from Martinsville High and head off to college at the University of Missouri. After Marian completed high school she would move to Kansas City to attend college. Upon entering the working world she held secretarial positions. She would marry Gene Bolin, and they would have three daughters, Gail, Jill, and Jane.

Very soon after moving to our second farm, I was observing farm duties in greater detail. The used and dirty water in the house was emptied into the sink and it would drain down into a large bucket on the floor underneath. For daily water use in the house on this farm Dad purchased a special ten-gallon can with a large lid firmly placed on top. It would be filled at a distant well. This required frequent trips in order to keep household water in proper supply.

Life was changing for me as a six-year old kid doing farm chores six days a week. On this farm, our windmill for filling the large livestock water tank was right at the edge of the barnyard. This was a far better water system for livestock than on the first farm. As I was now participating in more and more farm chores with each passing month as I was growing older and stronger and capable of helping with more and more farm duties my life was continuing to change with each passing year.

The water tank for the cattle and horses was filled with a long connection from the pump straight up to the top of the windmill. When the windmill was in the "on" position, the wind would rotate the circular structure at the top, and that provided the constant up-and-down pumping power needed to fill the water tank. When the tank was full, the windmill could be adjusted into "off" position. For this, someone had to be close by to observe when the water tank was full.

Horses and cattle roaming in the pasture could now get quickly get to the water tank at the windmill and get their water. For hogs or poultry, we had to carry water in three-gallon buckets to a ground-level trough. In the chicken house, there was a container that would be filled with water, and it would slowly flow as needed into the lower area for the chickens. There was something similar for our turkeys or ducks.

This was all part of morning and evening chores as I was growing up. Also the idea of having water from a faucet in the house was not yet even in our dreams. We could make our way to town or a nearby grocery store when required regardless of rain or snow. The graveled roadway along this second farm was professionally maintained, so it was passable every day regardless of weather. This was a great improvement over our first farm.

My father built a new house for us there. This house had a nice back porch on which the motorized washing machine was placed for my mother to do the regular clothes-washing duties. That was a nice update from the hand-powered system in our previous washing machine. When this was completed, the clothes were hung on the nearby line to dry. The garden was very close by our back door.

I remember the day Dad came home from Bethany driving a 1938 Chevrolet. This car was far more comfortable than the models of the late 1920s and earlier 1930s. In the winter months we now for the first time had a heater in the car. In earlier days, you just bundled up in the cold winter months so you would be warm and comfortable in your automobile.

Automobiles and tractors of the early 1930s required more regular maintenance and repair than the vehicles and equipment of today. There was a shop in Washington Center to our north and one in Martinsville to our south for repair of automobiles, tractors, and other farm equipment. Tractor repair was normally taken care of on the farm. It was not reasonable to drive our big steel-wheeled tractor to town for any repair work needed. On rare occasions, Dad would call a nearby mechanic who would drive to our farm and do the more complicated repair work necessary on the tractor.

We had a special large barrel where the local delivery truck would deliver gasoline for the tractor about once a month. It would be emptied into that barrel, and then from a spout into a special small bucket for filling the tractor gasoline tank.

Most of the farms in our surrounding area consisted of 160 to 240 acres. A few were larger. Getting all over the farm with the tractor was necessary in order to prepare the fields for crop planting. In addition to our Farmal tractor, a team of horses continued to be put to work six days a week.

Our wood-burning kitchen stove had a large level top surface and just below that was the sizable oven. It was accessed by way of a large oven door on the lower wide front side. There was need to carry wood to the back porch every day to provide fuel for the kitchen and front room stoves. Our principal source of fuel for the stoves was the woodpile. Dad was still chopping down trees and continuing the process of sawing and chopping wood into proper size for the kitchen and front room.

I was doing a bit more farm work year by year and soon started helping Dad with the crosscut saw. It was about six feet in length with a handle on each end. It required one person on each end of the saw drawing it back and forth to perform the sawing operation. It was used to saw down trees on the farm and then saw the limbs and branches off the large tree trunk. Some of the twigs and small branches were removed with an axe.

With this complete, the crosscut saw came into use again. The large tree trunks and branches were sawed into many pieces of wood about twelve inches in length. With this done, the large pieces would be split into pieces of wood small enough in diameter to use in the kitchen and front room stove.

Splitting a piece of wood twelve to sixteen inches in diameter would become one of my teenage duties. The splitting was done by placing a small iron wedge on top of an upright fourteen-inch-long piece of wood placed upright on the ground. A heavy sledgehammer was used to pound that wedge down, splitting that piece of wood. This would produce smaller pieces of wood appropriate in size for the wood-burning stoves in the house.

During the cold winter months, the chunks of wood were used in the large front room stove to provide heating for the house. Smaller chunks were used in the smaller kitchen stove year-round. We always had a large pile of wood near the back of the house. One of my regular evening chores was to carry the necessary chunks of wood to the back porch for use in the house every day.

We had no stoves in the bedrooms. We had heavy blankets and covers for the cold winter months when it was bedtime. The heat from the kitchen and front room stoves was sufficient to keep the downstairs reasonably warm in the winter months. The winter temperature in northern Missouri could get down to well below zero. Dad's first duty in the winter months was to arise early and get the stoves going to spread at least some warmth throughout the house.

In the 1930s, we began using coal for fuel and would order a load of coal to be brought to the farm. It would be emptied into our backyard. Buckets of coal would be brought daily to the back porch for both the kitchen and front room stoves. No more chopping wood required. I was now carrying the necessary buckets of coal for daily use in the house in all household stoves when I was eight years old. No more sawing down of trees on the farm was required.

Only the morning and evening chores were done on Sunday. There were beef cattle, dairy cattle, chickens, and hogs to be fed daily. I was now responsible for bringing the feed and water to the chicken house or the area where we had a few turkeys.

On this second farm, the main barn was somewhat smaller than the one on the first farm. Therefore, Dad built another barn very close by in the barn lot to serve as our dairy barn. We now had stanchions to keep the dairy cows firmly in place when evening milking time came. We were milking eight to ten dairy cows daily. I was old enough to be of moderate assistance when milking time came each evening. All you had to do was put a bit of feed for the dairy cows in the trough area and then open the barn door, and the dairy cows would quickly come from the lot into the barn. They would go to their individual stalls and be secured.

By the time I reached fifth grade, I was capable of helping with virtually all farm duties and could almost keep up with Dad at milking time. I was learning and understanding much more about daily farm life. My boyhood hands were becoming larger and stronger with each passing year.

We consumed a lot of nutritious milk. We had a Separator for use in separating cream from the milk fresh from the dairy cows. I was now the one turning the Separator crank around and around producing the power to operate this piece of equipment. On top of the Separator was a bowl into which the buckets of fresh milk from the dairy barn would be poured. Turning the crank on the side would rotate the equipment and this would separate the cream from the milk.

Out one small spout would come the cream, and out another larger spout would come the larger supply of what we referred to as skimmed milk. That was the milk we drank three meals a day. Any excess milk would be taken to a hog trough.

We would place some cream into our special small churn and this would produce butter. Excess cream not needed in the kitchen was placed in a cream can. Once each week this five-gallon can of cream would be taken to a local store where it was tested for butterfat level. With that process completed a slip of paper would be taken to the cash register at the front of the store stating the value of your cream and also the eggs from our flock of hens.

Once each month we would drive to the nearby larger town of Bethany and the farm income checks would be taken to the bank for deposit. There were several shops and stores there. Nearby Martinsville and Washington Center were not large enough to have a bank. The cream and egg money was an important part of our income but the major portion of income was from the sale of livestock.

Chapter 27

MORE ABOUT FARM LIFE AND ON TO HIGH SCHOOL IN 1942

M ORE FARM CHORES WERE BEING added to my schedule each year. Soon we had a new farm tractor. It had rubber tires and a starter. No more steel-wheeled tractor for us, and no more tractor cranking required. This was in the late 1940s, and we were living on our second farm about four miles to the north of Martinsville.

There was a small country store about three miles to the north of our farm at Washington Center. In addition to that, there was a blacksmith repair shop for cars and farm equipment. There was also the Washington Center one-room country school. Dad and Mom would travel frequently to this village store to sell our cream and egg products and to do the necessary purchase of grocery items.

In Martinsville, there were two churches, a grocery store, and a small restaurant. The grocery store on the north side of the street was the John Graham Store. Next to it was the post office. Soon a second store opened on the south side of the street. Just a couple of blocks to the south of downtown Martinsville there was the large red brick school building. There was first grade through eighth grade and then on to high school all in one brick building.

I was now accompanying Dad to the grocery store and observing more closely the weekly shopping duties. After completing eighth grade at the one room Long Branch country school, I was soon accompanying my brother and sisters on the school bus ride to Martinsville High School. Going from the small one-room country school to a large brick building with dozens more students than I was familiar with was a significant change in my life.

I was old enough now to be working occasionally for neighboring farmers and coming home with a small check or a dollar bill or two. My bank account balance in Bethany was continuing to grow. It had been established to produce the income that would provide funds required for my college education.

In my first week of high school as I exited the bus one evening my mother met me at the door and said, "Dad is down at the barn lot. He wants to talk to you."

As I approached the barn lot, I observed that it was full of sheep. We had never had any sheep before, only cattle, horses, and hogs. Dad met me at the edge of the barn lot and with a cheerful smile said to me, "Look here, Gerald, this is your herd of sheep. This is what will provide your own personal income to cover your college education."

That is one of my most vivid lifetime memories. I was now responsible for all the feeding and caring required for that herd of thirty sheep. Very soon into my high school freshman year, I was off to the Kansas City American Royal to show my lambs and calf in competition. This was a major livestock event. To my complete surprise, my beef calf placed very high. I would also end up in the championship category with my lambs.

My livestock income continued to grow successfully for the next four years. Every penny went into my bank account, and this income later covered all expenses for my college education at the University of Missouri.

There were only ten in my high school class in Martinsville and I was soon on the basketball team. Before that, I had never even touched a basketball. In my junior and senior years in 1945 and 1946, my basketball skills continued to develop.

William Booth was our high school superintendent and basketball coach. Other team members included Jim Kidwell, Myron Mock, Gayle Hook, Jim Runyan, Charles Terry, Bill Butler, Rex Lyon, Harold Hook, and Melvin Eckard. We were doing reasonably well with other small-town teams throughout the Harrison and Gentry County area in northwest Missouri. In my senior high school year we were competing in the Albany

Basketball Tournament for the smaller towns of the area. This was 1946 and we were playing the Amity High School team for the championship. We struggled our way into the fourth quarter and were leading by two points. On one of our possessions the opposing team stole the ball from us and scored. That tied the game.

Then we were attempting to score and they stole the ball from us again and one of their players was dribbling down court well ahead of everyone and apparently ready to make an easy two points. That would have put them in the lead. However, I had learned the little trick of staying far enough back in this kind of situation that he would not be aware that I was even close by.

He went up gently for what he thought would be an easy two points. When he did that, I suddenly sped up and jumped high, hitting that basketball with my fist before it reached the basket. It slammed onto the brick wall on the side of the court and bounced back clear across the court and up into the spectator area on the other side above court level. I heard many "oohs" coming from those in attendance.

We played well for another few minutes and won the Albany tournament championship. That was the pinnacle of my athletic career. I even stole the ball once from the opposing team and dribbled down for my certain two points.

I have in my files a letter that was written after this tournament by our high school superintendent and basketball coach, William E. Booth. At this time, I was known as Gerald Carter. Mr. Booth's letter starts with the heading "Martinsville High Squad 1945-1946" and reads as follows:

> Sixteen strong squads, efficient officials, keen competition. Gayle Hook captained the squad thru the last three crucial games, kept a level head and bore the brunt of the goal defense. Suffice it to say he did the job and did it well. Gerald Carter directed the team offense, used his head and did anticipatory thinking and bore into the opposition with fury in times of crises.
>
> In the final game, first overtime, he made the shot that tied the game and in the second overtime charged

into an airtight defense, stole the ball and dribbled down court to fire the winning sudden death shot.

Myron Mock led the offense with speed and stellar shooting accuracy. Although a marked man struggling against unusual odds he topped the list in points for his squad. Charles Terry utilized his floor speed, keen eye, evasive tactics and with his unerring shooting ability pulled us out of several serious situations and demoralized the opposition with seemingly impossible corner shots.

Bill Butler was always "in there" giving his best and supporting his teammates and showed instantaneous judgment on two occasions in applying defensive tactics when we were trailing and they froze the ball. This lightning action on his part confused the opposition and enabled us to recover the ball when we were fighting with our backs to the wall.

Rex Lyon was aggressive with the ability to take a dangerous goal artist of the opposition out of circulation and hold him scoreless for several minutes of play enabling Myron Mock and Charles Terry to devote more time to the offense. Melvin Eckard, who filled the gap on several occasions, used superior judgment in the application of speed and faking in the support of his teammates.

In twenty years of coaching I have never had a squad of boys who tried more earnestly to follow the instructions of their coach. I especially commend them on a level headedness, continuous endeavor and the "never say die" fighting spirit. To the Student Body at Martinsville High School I say they are deserving and worthy. They are a credit to your school. Give them your enthusiastic support."

—*William Booth, coach, Martinsville High*

In addition to the athletic side of my high school years, I was doing well in my studies and would graduate as valedictorian of my very small senior class. During these high school years, I was also assisting my father and brother in all farm duties. In 1946 after high school graduation, I was off to the University of Missouri and back on the farm only in the summer months.

Chapter 28

MY BROTHER ROBERT CARTER AND HIS EXPERIENCE AT THE BATTLE OF THE BULGE IN WORLD WAR II

HITLER STARTED WORLD WAR II in 1939 and was on his way to conquer Europe. My older brother Robert had graduated from Martinsville High School and was in college at the University of Missouri. He was immediately drafted into the army in his second college year. After a brief intensive basic training his unit was off to the European theater of operations.

One day soon after that terrible war was won, I had a quiet conversation with Robert on our farm as we looked out over the open fields from our back porch. He was safely in home country and on furlough. There were many soldiers in that war and it was taking time to properly release all of them from the army. I was in my early teenage years at this time.

It was a beautiful morning, and the sun was just rising over a distant hillside. Following is a brief report on his personal experience in one of the major battles of that war. Robert gave me the details of that battle as he lived it.

Hitler's army was driving from Germany on westward into Europe. There was no major nation the size of the United States with population sufficient to put a stop to Hitler's surging army. He was obviously on his way to conquer a major area of Europe. For the Allied forces General Dwight Eisenhower's army was defending a position that would become known as the Battle of the Bulge.

Robert and two other young soldiers were forward observers for the artillery unit that was part of General Eisenhower's army in Western Europe. They knew Hitler's army was advancing in their general direction.

The duty of these three forward observers was to send a message back to their artillery unit if they detected any activity far ahead of their front line that would require immediate artillery firing. Communication was by way of a landline—a telephone line strewn along on the ground connecting them with their unit a few hundred yards back.

They knew Hitler's army was moving in their direction. They did not have information as to precisely where it was. He and his buddies were on duty twenty-four hours a day—an eight-hour shift for each. That is the only way they could sleep or have time to get the food that was brought to them from their front line.

Technology of that time called for the artillery unit to be ready to fire upon receipt of information from these three forward observers as to any enemy movement they observed. If they saw any movement they were to immediately send a message by way of the telephone line. The artillery unit was to fire three times.

The first artillery firing was to be at least slightly beyond the approaching enemy. Robert and his buddies were to send the message back to their artillery commander as to where the first shot landed relative to the intended target. The next firing was to be slightly closer. With details provided by these forward observers, the third firing was intended to be on target. This was distant artillery firing in World War II.

One day very soon after deployment to this site, Robert and his two buddies saw Hitler's army crashing suddenly over a distant hillside in massive numbers. The observers had to transmit that message to their unit immediately. That was successfully done, and then their order was to destroy their equipment. With that accomplished, they were to get back to safety. They knew their lives were in immediate danger.

However, before they could get back to safety, these three young college-age boys were captured by Hitler's surging forces and were being escorted off to prison by five German soldiers. Logic tells us that they would have been the first prisoners captured by Hitler's army there at the Battle of the Bulge. Many more in my brother's unit would soon be captured.

According to the story Robert told me about their capture, they were given the order, *"No talk."* The first day and night they observed the overnight procedure. The five enemy soldiers were spending the night in shifts so each would have time for food and so they all could get some sleep.

Robert and his buddies received no food and no water. They decided and somehow communicated without saying a word that they would stay awake and escape during the second night. In my young teenage way, as this conversation was taking place, I blurted out, "And did you?"

He hesitated and then turned to me slowly and said very quietly, "Yes."

I could tell by his slow and solemn answer that this was a very serious memory for him. He confirmed that they carefully made their way back to the safety of the Allied line. Those fifteen minutes when Robert was telling me this story remain as one of my most vivid life memories.

Based on the information he related to me, it is my conclusion that Robert and his two buddies should have been declared the heroes of the Battle of the Bulge. It was their communication from a dangerous distance ahead of the front line that gave Eisenhower and the Allied forces several minutes of warning that Hitler's army was fast approaching.

Another soldier who was on the frontline and captured was Hal Taylor. I met him on campus at the University of Missouri just after the war, and we became friends. He told me about his experience at the Battle of the Bulge. After capture, Hal and many others were escorted to a railway line and loaded into cattle cars. They were sitting on the floor of the cattle cars on their way to prison.

Hal has written a book about his experience at the Battle of the Bulge and as a prisoner of war in World War II. The cover of his book reads, *A Teen's War—Training, Combat, Capture* by Hal Richard Taylor. It has proven to be a very popular book on what battle was really like in World War II. I have asked friends who have studied the history of World War II from books available in university and public libraries if they recalled any of these details on this battle.

I have come to the conclusion that my friend Hal Taylor's book is the most complete and personal book available on the history of World War

II. Hal and my brother were there. They didn't have to do any research. It was all in their vivid memory.

General Eisenhower's army would soon gain control. The Allied army was advancing driving Hitler and his army back into Germany. Robert was no longer on the front line. He was assigned to a unit that was providing food for those communities devastated by Hitler's army movement westward and then back into Germany.

Robert had one more interesting story to tell me when he was safely back in the allied line area Soon the war was over and he was released from the army and had a very brief story to tell me about one of one his last days in service.

He told me of being armed with a holstered pistol as he was carefully overseeing the food line in one of those totally devastated German neighborhoods. The local German citizens were friendly and grateful for the food being provided. That is the way it was until one day he received a serious nod from one of the local German citizens just across the food line. The crew had been provided information that Hitler was organizing teenage boys and convincing them that "his way" was the only way.

The serious nod from this person caused Robert to swivel immediately around to find a young lad just a few feet away with a pistol bringing it down on him. Robert took care of the problem. This was the last conversation I ever had with my brother about his experiences in World War II. That was obviously not a fond memory for him.

After army discharge Robert returned to the University of Missouri and completed his college education. He married Helen, a young lady he had met while in the armed services and they had a son, Greg, and a daughter, Patti. He obtained employment with Farmland Industries in Kansas City and enjoyed a very successful management position there for the rest of his working career. Farmland Industries would become a major corporation owned by approximately 600,000 investors.

I have searched but never found any mention of those three first prisoners captured by Hitler's army and their return to safety in any coverage of the Battle of the Bulge.

Chapter 29

OFF TO THE UNIVERSITY OF MISSOURI FOR ME IN 1946

A FTER I GRADUATED FROM MARTINSVILLE High School in 1946 my father was responsible for all farm labor. I was now attending the University of Missouri in Columbia, enrolled in the College of Agriculture, Food, and Natural Resources. During the summer months, I would be back on the farm to help Dad with the farm duties.

I added the School of Journalism to my schedule and therefore would graduate with two degrees, one from the College of Agriculture and the other from the School of Journalism. Currently, *US News and World Report* ranks the University of Missouri School of Journalism as the number one journalism school in America.

I became a member of the Alpha Gamma Sigma fraternity where my brother Robert was a member. He introduced me to others on campus as his brother Jerry Carter. Before that, I was always Gerald Carter to friends and family. Soon I was known on the MU campus as Jerry. I have been known since that time as Jerry Carter. Officially, I remain William Gerald Carter. My Alpha Gamma Sigma fraternity would be my place of residence for my college years.

The first two chapters for this fraternity had been the Alpha Chapter at Ohio University and my Beta Chapter at the University of Missouri. Later at one of our fraternity reunions those attending were Don Neiderhauser, Al Specker, Bob Witten, Bob King, Kenneth Haynes, Lloyd Doane, and one of the Barrett twins, Robert or Richard. A photo was taken of those in attendance. College professors in the photo who also had attended the University of Missouri and had been members of Alpha Gamma Sigma included Elmer Kiehl and Woody Woodruff. Elmer Kiehl would go on to major accomplishments nationwide.

In my first college year, I joined the *College Farmer* student magazine staff. Hal Taylor was the editor. I would soon serve as editor of this fine student magazine. This campus activity turned out to be a major part of my journalism education. This was a successful and professional student magazine on the University of Missouri campus.

I was invited to join the college honor society known as QEBH. This resulted from my participation in positions of student leadership throughout the University of Missouri campus. Also on my list of college honor society memberships is Omicron Delta Kappa. In that organization are some famous individuals, including former US Congressman Ike Skelton and Sam Walton, founder of the highly successful Walmart store chain. In my senior year, I received notice that I was now listed in *Who's Who Among Students in American Colleges and Universities.*

After college graduation when I was no longer available to return and help Dad on the farm, my parents sold our farm and moved to nearby Bethany in northwest Missouri. Dad obtained employment in the housing construction profession for he had considerable experience building houses, barns, and other farm buildings.

Chapter 30

LIFE AFTER COLLEGE: MY FIRST JOB AND THE KOREAN WAR

AFTER GRADUATING FROM THE UNIVERSITY of Missouri in 1950 I learned from a friend that there was a job opening in Chicago with the *National Livestock Producer* magazine. I was familiar with that publication. My father was a subscriber, and I had been reading it for several years. Thinking my college education in both journalism and agriculture would qualify me for the job, I immediately applied.

I was invited to come to Chicago for a personal interview, made the trip, and was accepted for the position of assistant editor of this magazine. In 1950, Mr. P. O. Wilson was the executive vice president of the National Livestock Producers Association.

I had never been in a city of this size, much less living there and commuting by public transportation to an office in the heart of downtown every day. For this country boy, living in Chicago was a major learning experience.

I rented a one-room apartment to the south of downtown Chicago. I was on the commuter train five days a week along with thousands of others. It was a twenty-minute walk from my apartment to the commuter train station. That was a very interesting experience for a farm boy.

My three daily meals were from small inexpensive restaurants near my apartment or the downtown Chicago office. The friendly couple who owned the house where I was living would often invite me to join them for Sunday dinner.

Life in downtown Chicago was not only a world of difference from life on the farm, but it was also nothing like life in Columbia, Missouri, when I was in college there. I was now researching and writing major articles for this magazine with substantial rural circulation throughout middle America. I traveled frequently in order to research and take photos for illustration. For the photos, I utilized a large speed graphic camera. My transportation was by bus, train, taxi, and occasionally rented automobile. I could not yet afford to purchase an automobile.

Today, the National Livestock Producers Association has no published magazine. However, there is a website with information available on the organization and how it operates today. It now serves more than 150,000 livestock producers throughout the United States. Multiply that by the fifty to two hundred head of livestock produced by each, and it gives you a clearer picture of the farms and rural population that the organization serves throughout America.

I recently had an interesting telephone conversation with a staff person at the National Livestock Producers Association, now headquartered in Colorado. The organization today is far larger than it was when I was employed there in the early 1950s.

In retrospect, I consider this first job a part of my continuing education. Daily chores of farm life were now history. Never again would I be milking cows and driving a team of horses or a tractor. It was the beginning of my experience with the practical side of the journalism profession, as well as my first taste of what city life was really like. My bank account began to slowly increase.

Soon I was drafted into the army, as the Korean War was under way at the time. There was serious disagreement between North Korea and South Korea. The United States chose to assist South Korea in defending its territory.

My basic training was in Missouri. During that time, those who had graduated from college were called in for a major test. At first, they did not tell us why. The test was very difficult. Soon thereafter, a few of us were called in again and informed that we had qualified for transfer into the intelligence section of the US Army. Our training would be at Fort Holabird, Maryland.

Before we were on our way to training, I observed my army unit boarding a train and heading for the West Coast. They were on their way to the Korean War, and I was on my way to training for service in the army counterintelligence corps. There were many casualties during that war. Some of my comrades were captured early in the war and spent time in a Korean prison. I was very fortunate to serve my army career safely in the United States in the early 1950s in this intelligence organization.

We had been informed that after our intelligence training, we could be sent overseas for duty or, if married, assigned within the United States. Geralyn Finlay (who attended Stephens College in Columbia, Missouri) and I were enjoying a loving relationship, and a wedding was held during a brief military furlough. Then we were off to Maryland for my intelligence training.

Those of us who made it through training were given an allowance to purchase business attire. We were to appear as normal citizens when we were out in the business world doing background checks on anyone who might be given access to United States classified information. Our final question in each interview was: "Would you approve this person for a position where they would have access to classified information?"

The usual answer was yes. There were only a few occasions when the answer was no. That information was passed on for further investigation and action if necessary by the United States intelligence agency.

I was first assigned to the office in St. Louis, Missouri. After a short time, I was assigned to cover a territory in the Decatur, Illinois area. My wife and I spent two years there. I would spend the remainder of my time in military service in civilian attire as a special agent in the United States intelligence service.

Our first daughter, Kathy, was born in Decatur. Her birthplace is a constant reminder to me that I qualified for entry into the United States intelligence service and was assigned to duty within the United States. Some of my army friends lost their lives in the Korean War. After that war, I was called in and advised of the opportunity to remain in the US intelligence service.

My immediate question was, "Where might I be assigned?" The reply was that it could be anywhere in the United States or possibly overseas. After careful consideration, I declined the opportunity. It seemed to me that my wife and I would prefer to be the ones deciding where we would be living.

Chapter 31

ARMY DISCHARGE AND RETURN TO JOURNALISM

A FTER I WAS DISCHARGED FROM the army in 1953 we moved to Kansas City rather than back to my Chicago job. My former boss in Chicago was not happy with that decision—the job had been held open for me during my military career. There was opportunity for employment in the public relations department at Farmland Industries in Kansas City, Missouri. I applied for this job and was accepted.

We were now living much closer to family and friends in my home state of Missouri. This company would become a major corporate entity in the United States. My wife and I purchased our first home in Kansas City. My brother held a management position at Farmland, and he and his family enjoyed a successful life in Kansas City. We would frequently drive on weekends to visit my parents, grandparents, or other friends and relatives in the relatively nearby Bethany area.

In this employment position, I traveled throughout the Midwest researching and preparing items for inclusion in a publication that was being distributed to employees and customers of Farmland Industries. The company would eventually serve more than 600,000 farm families, with a gross income well into the millions of dollars.

A few years later a friend of mine called to inform me of another job in which I might be interested. This was with the Missouri Farmer's Association, with an office in Columbia. I checked it out, and it would be a step up in compensation. It was a public relations position. After careful consideration we decided to make the move.

When looking for a place to live in Columbia, I received a call from a college friend advising that there was a house nearby to the north of Columbia that had just come on the market. We checked it out, purchased it, and would live there for the next seven years. Our new location included about ten acres of land. There was a small storage shed and a pond. I would invest in a few head of calves each year, grow them to maturity, and sell them at a profit. It reminded me of my years on the farm.

This was nothing like a major investment, but it was making use of that land and did produce a modest income. We would plant our first garden at this location. Our second daughter, Karen, was born there, and our first daughter, Kathy, began first grade at a nearby one-room country school.

Chapter 32

JOINING THE GRANT NEDS AND BERNIE WARDLOW ADVERTISING AGENCY

A FTER SEVEN YEARS OF EMPLOYMENT in Columbia would come an invitation from friends in the journalism profession, Grant Neds and Bernie Wardlow, to become a partner in their successful advertising agency. Their office was in Kansas City and they were ready to expand. I accepted the invitation. I was asked to move to the growing city of Springfield, Missouri to open an office there. Corporately, the company was known as the Neds and Wardlow Advertising Agency.

At that time the city of Springfield was experiencing expansion and the commercial side of life presented an opportunity. Other cities in the area were also growing and area businesses needed help with the advertising and public relations side of their operation. My office was in one of John Q. Hammons's properties. I had to deliver my monthly office rental payment to his office nearby. Mr. Hammons would go on to outstanding success in the real estate investment profession building many Holiday Inns in America.

As a partner in the Neds and Wardlow agency, I would make an appointment with an area corporate office and advise them as to how we could be of assistance to them in their advertising and promotions. If they accepted and agreed to become a client, I would prepare the advertising and promotional material required. It could include radio, television, or newspaper advertising, or some combination of the three.

Monthly media cost was calculated along with the necessary preparation charges. With client approval, we would prepare the advertising copy and then complete a contract with the media. In addition, I would frequently submit news releases for area media on news items related to my clientele. Sometimes there was an opportunity to publicize an important community activity that a client was responsible for. This was the public relations side of our service.

I was soon successfully serving businesses located throughout southwest Missouri, northwest Arkansas, and northeast Oklahoma. I would prepare all material and send newspaper or magazine advertising copy off to our Kansas City office for Bernie Wardlow to do the necessary layout and artwork required. Radio and television advertising I was able to take care of locally.

My client list was steadily growing. One day, when searching for additional clients, I stopped in and visited with Mr. Sam Walton. His office was a few miles to the south of Springfield in northwest Arkansas. Walton had just started the Walmart Super Center operation in 1962. His office at that time was in a very small red brick building, and he shared his cramped space with two secretarial assistants. I asked if I could have a brief visit with Mr. Walton.

He was available. I entered his office and introduced myself as a partner in the Neds and Wardlow Advertising Agency. I explained briefly the services we offered, and then I asked if we could be of assistance in advertising and promoting his relatively small Walmart operation. He very kindly declined, saying he already had that side of the business taken care of.

That would later turn out to be one of the most memorable business appointments of my career. At that time, his office was only modestly larger than the very small office from which I was operating. Walmart was just getting started. A few years later, it was obvious that his company was growing by leaps and bounds.

Today, Walmart is reported to be one of the largest corporations in the world. They employ more than two million associates at ten thousand stores in twenty-nine countries. Annual sales volume is now in the billions of dollars. I am proud just to have had a personal and friendly conversation with the famous Mr. Sam Walton.

Chapter 33

LIFE IN SPRINGFIELD, MISSOURI AND IN OKLAHOMA CITY

L IFE IN SPRINGFIELD, MISSOURI WAS challenging and very interesting. I became district chairman and member of the executive committee of the Ozark Empire Area Boy Scouts of America. For these accomplishments, I received notice that I had been chosen to receive the local distinguished service award in 1963.

I also became a member of the Junior Chamber of Commerce, a philanthropic organization of young men under the age of thirty-six and I was engaged at that time in promoting the successful careers of the younger generation. We would soon simplify the name of the organization to the Jaycees. I became president of my local club. Thanks to my leadership in this organization I was selected as Springfield's Young Man of the Year in 1963.

After a successful career with the Neds and Wardlow Advertising Agency I sold that facility and founded Tri State Pharmaceutical Company. That required purchasing prescription medications from manufacturing firms and calling on physicians to seek their support in utilizing my prescription medications. We were expanding and soon moved to relatively nearby Oklahoma City. I was purchasing products from the Sun Belt manufacturing facility with headquarters in Atlanta, Georgia.

Eventually came the opportunity to sell the Tri State Pharmaceutical Company at a comfortable profit to the Sun Belt organization. I was asked to serve in a management position at this major facility. This would require a move to Georgia. After careful consideration, my wife and I made the decision to accept sale of the company but remain in our friendly neighborhood in Oklahoma.

We were enjoying a fine life with family and friends. I was now also investing in real estate. I would purchase vacant houses, duplexes and apartment complexes in need of relatively minor repair, fix them up, and place them on the market for sale. Very soon we had seventy rental units. That was my full-time daily duty to do all utility necessary to keep all properties in attractive, comfortable condition. With that many units, there would be occasional vacancies, and that required repair and painting. This was a busy and quite successful real estate investment career for me.

Chapter 34

ON TO LEADERSHIP IN THE OPTIMIST INTERNATIONAL ORGANIZATION THEN INDUCTED INTO *WHO'S WHO IN AMERICA*

I SOON BECAME A MEMBER OF the Optimist International organization. We were now living in Oklahoma City where I would become president of my Oklahoma City Optimist Club.

A problem soon became evident with the membership level of the Oklahoma Optimist International District. Our membership was down and no one was stepping up to serve as our Oklahoma District Governor. Even though I was relatively new in the organization I was asked if I would accept the governor position and I did. A visiting national officer emphatically suggested that we get out and build new clubs to get our membership up to a higher level.

We took that challenge seriously, and our membership in Oklahoma began growing immediately thanks to the efforts of members throughout the district. We were having special meetings to spread the word that we must continue to get our membership up to a more comfortable level. With much effort by members throughout Oklahoma, we started to see strong growth. Additional clubs were organized throughout our district and the membership of individual clubs increased. The future of the Oklahoma district was assured. We had grown from twenty struggling clubs to more than thirty strong clubs in only a few years.

My wife and I were now attending Optimist International conventions at various cities every two years throughout the United States and Canada, and I was soon serving on committees at the international level. I was appointed to serve as chairman of the Optimist International membership committee. After reasonable success in that committee, it was on to chairmanship of the international convention committee.

Usually there would be more than one city in America or Canada competing to host the convention. We had to collect information about each potential site in order to make our selection. As chairman, I reviewed this information in detail and then presented it to our committee. After further study, we would make the decision as to which location would be best for that coming year. Next I would present our committee proposal to the Optimist International board of directors for approval. The board would make the final decision as to where the upcoming convention would be held.

Following my time on the convention committee came a move to the position of vice president of Optimist International. It has always been a great comfort for me to know that this prestigious organization is one of the major organizations at a national and international level serving our communities in a positive manner.

Another committee I was involved with was the one promoting oratorical contests. We encouraged clubs to have public speaking contests for high school students to help them develop their skills in making verbal presentations to sizable groups. With my journalism background, I suggested to the international board of directors that we should also have an essay contest. For me it was just as important to promote the ability to create a properly "written document" as it was to encourage development of public speaking skills among young students.

The board of directors agreed, and the Optimist International Essay Contest project was under way. I became the first chairman of this committee, and we established the guidelines and instructions for clubs to follow in sponsoring this activity.

In a recent telephone conversation with Optimist International staff, I asked if the essay contest was continuing successfully. The answer was a definite yes. I soon received a small octagonal bronze medallion that reads "Optimist International Essay Contest." This is the medallion that is presented to local high school Essay-Contest winners each year throughout the United States and Canada.

I was recently informed that the Essay Contest is now the second most popular activity in the Optimist International organization. High school winners receive college scholarships. I remember the details I went through when I became chairman of this newly established committee to prepare those original instructions and guidelines.

This is the current essay medallion. It is presented to local winners of the Optimist International Essay Contest.

While all these activities were under way, to my complete surprise, I received notification that I had been chosen for listing in *Who's Who in America*. I was asked for verification of the information they had prepared regarding all community leadership categories in which I had served. It was complete and accurate, and so I gave the verification. Very soon thereafter, I received official notification that I was now listed in **Who's Who in America** for leadership activities in the not-for-profit sector of the US economy.

Chapter 35

OUR MOVE TO CALIFORNIA AND INVOLVEMENT IN THE OVY CAMP ORGANIZATION

A N OPPORTUNITY CAME FOR A move from Oklahoma to California in 1987. All our real estate investment properties were sold at a comfortable profit. In California, I continued successfully in the commercial real estate profession as a broker, listing and selling commercial properties. We were living in Foster City, which is about midway between San Francisco and San Jose. We were only a few miles from the Pacific coast.

After our arrival in California, when I was searching for additional commercial properties to list and place on the market, I saw a billboard that read, "Boys and Girlsville Pioneer Village." That seemed interesting to me, and I checked it out further.

Many years before, the property had been the residence of a local Optimist Club member. He did not have family to leave the property to when he passed away, so he prepared official documents stating that upon his passing, his eighty acres of land would go to Optimist members living in the San Francisco to San Jose area. He directed that it be established as a summer camp for the boys and girls of the area whose parents could not afford to send their children to more expensive facilities.

I immediately joined the fine organization overseeing this property, Optimist Volunteers for Youth (OVY), and the Boys and Girlsville Pioneer Village would soon become the OVY Camp and Event Center. Many

Optimist members and others throughout the area are active as volunteers in the operation of this beautiful eighty-acre rural facility in central California. The camp required employees on site twenty-four hours a day year-round.

When the four-week summer camping sessions for the young boys and girls of the area are completed, the camp is open to the public for the remainder of the year. It serves as a special corporate-function facility or a rural vacation facility. Those attending a vacationing event knew that the money they are charged will go toward keeping the camp in pristine condition.

The temperature at this location in California was comfortable throughout the year. It was never hot and never cold. Along with many others, I was spending many volunteer hours collecting donations to provide the funding necessary for operation of this unusual facility. With continuing community effort, we obtained sufficient funding to successfully operate the OVY Camp and Event Center.

There was a lot of work involved in maintaining the property, including mowing the grassland in the cabin areas and maintaining the lengthy hiking trails throughout the facility. There were a lot of weeds growing in this rural area requiring a lot of attention. In the central office there is a fine kitchen and large dining hall for three meals a day. Camp operation requires many volunteer hours in addition to the management staff on duty twenty-four hours a day.

Soon I was on the board of directors and elected to the position of secretary. Many in the organization were donating both time and money to keep the camp bank account at a reasonable level. One day I received a telephone call from an Optimist member in nearby San Jose who was also a member of the Veterans of Foreign Wars organization. He told me they had a large professional bingo hall for their own fund-raising purpose and that it was leased out to other not-for-profit organizations on certain evenings of the month.

He advised me that there would soon be a vacancy occurring and suggested that our organization should consider sponsoring a bingo night. He assured me this would provide substantial income for the permanent successful operation of our OVY Camp organization. As secretary of that organization, I drove immediately to San Jose to check it out.

I was impressed with the size and professional equipment available at this facility. There were many men and women attending the weekly bingo nights. They could enjoy an evening with friends and neighbors knowing that they were providing necessary income for successful operation of their local VFW retirement facility. They also knew there would be a chance to get a bingo and win a comfortable sum for themselves.

Upon arrival, the players registered, purchased their bingo cards for the evening, and proceeded to one of the tables distributed throughout the large facility. It had capacity for many players. Management personnel confirmed to me that there would soon be a night available for rental to another not-for-profit organization to sponsor a fund-raising bingo night. They suggested that we should respond quickly for there were other not for profit organizations in the area familiar with the facility.

I made several calls to members of our OVY board of directors. No one was available. At that time, our group was not yet officially registered as a not for profit organization at California state level. This was a requirement for this fund-raiser. As an officially elected officer of the organization I took it upon myself to drive to the state capitol in Sacramento and complete the process of registering the OVY as a not for profit organization.

With that accomplished, I again contacted members of the board to tell them what I had done. They enthusiastically supported my actions, and our agreement with the bingo facility was now complete. Our own regular bingo night would soon begin. Many Optimist members in the area drove to this facility in San Jose several evenings a month to observe and learn the process of sponsoring and conducting our bingo night.

When our own OVY bingo night started our bank balance immediately began to grow. Players were charged a modest fee for their evening of relaxation and a chance to win a few dollars. They knew that regardless of whether they won or lost, they were in essence donating money to the VFW facility or to the not-for-profit organization that was sponsoring that particular evening of bingo. The sponsoring organization received a sizable portion of the evening income.

Volunteers at the entry table officially registered those arriving and collected the modest charge. After the official bingo caller announced the number called into the public address system, it is entered into an electronic system and immediately readable high on the wall of the large professional facility.

When a player makes a bingo call one of the volunteers immediately goes to the lucky player's table, takes the player's bingo sheet and reads precisely what is on the player's card. When confirmed as correct, the bingo winner receives his or her cash prize for that game.

At the end of the evening there would be a check for our percentage of income for that evening. As secretary of our organization, I would take the proceeds received from each night of bingo and deposit into our bank account. This would quickly become the major income source for the operation of the OVY camp.

Many now spend vacation time at this beautiful rural not-for-profit facility. The temperature there is comfortable year-round. Vacations can be any length of time that fits a family's schedule. The camp is but a short drive from the Pacific shoreline where one can watch huge five and six foot waves constantly crashing. It is far too dangerous to consider even wading into the Pacific Ocean here, but the scenic view is outstanding and draws many families to come and enjoy from a spot safely back on shore. Since the camp is about midway between San Francisco and San Jose, either or both of those major cities can be visited during vacation time.

There are comfortable, unusual individual cabins for overnight vacation stay. There is a large playground area and a fine swimming pool for children and adults. All necessary information for booking a vacation can be obtained by going to your computer and logging on to **www. ovycamp.org**. The OVY mission reads, "It is our mission to provide youth with a safe, enjoyable and educational camping experience while offering character building opportunities and promoting service, volunteerism and leadership within the community."

One of my special memories is the day we received a letter from a lady asking for more information about the camp. She did not list her telephone number, but her return address was on the envelope. I drove to her house and learned that she had heard about the camp and had a young son she wanted to send for a summer-camp experience.

After explaining the details and telling her about the registration process and the cost, I asked her if she would like to register her son for a week of summer OVY camp. She said, "Yes, but I have no way of getting him to camp. I do not own an automobile." I immediately told her I would come by and pick him up and get him to camp.

Several days later, when the summer camp session was ready to begin, I drove to her house, and her son was ready and waiting. The mother asked again what the cost for the camp was. I told her it would be only ten dollars. I could hear and observe that she was looking everywhere for money in the kitchen cabinets, the bedroom, and elsewhere. Finally she started sobbing and said, "I don't have ten dollars."

I told her a check would be okay. Her reply to that was "I don't have a checking account." I told her I would take care of it.

The boy was very quiet on our way to camp. Hardly a word was spoken. Upon arrival, I helped him with the necessary registration procedure and paid his camping fee. The mother did not have a telephone, so I listed my address and telephone number in case there was any reason during the week that they would need to reach the family. That is standard procedure.

As usual, I was volunteering along with other OVY members during the ensuing camping week and I continued to observe how the young lad was doing. Everything was going well with no problems. He was active, happy, and enjoying every hour of every day with all the other campers. They were enjoying the hiking trails, swimming pool, and scenic rural land, along with other games, activities, and three meals a day.

When the week was up I drove to camp to pick the boy up and take him home. I asked if he had enjoyed his week. That young lad who hadn't said anything to me when I'd driven him to camp was so excited about his week of activities that our conversation was constant. He told me in great detail all the wonderful things he had done and what a great time he'd had. Seeing this particular result of the volunteer hours provided by many individuals of the area remains one of the great memories of my life.

Some of the cabins have a name on them to honor individuals who have made substantial monetary donations or provided special leadership important to the successful operation of the camp. I was very pleased and surprised one day when advised that there is now a cabin with my name on it.

I have a small plaque that is always on my desk. It reads: "William G. Carter, Founder OVY Bingo." That is the most prized trophy of my life for this bingo operation assures that there will be income necessary for the successful permanent operation of this fine OVY facility.

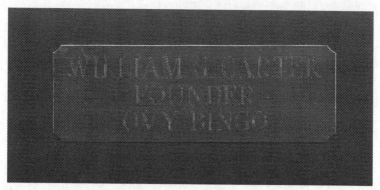

William G. Carter, Founder OVY Bingo.

I read that plaque 365 days a year. It is a constant reminder to me of the great service rendered by many who volunteer as well as the staff employees on duty seven days a week year-round at the OVY Camp. Through the years, thousands of boys, girls, and adults have benefited from this not-for-profit vacation facility.

Chapter 36

RETIREMENT AND RETURN TO MY HOME STATE OF MISSOURI

AFTER SPENDING SEVERAL SUCCESSFUL YEARS as a real estate broker in California and enjoying occasional trips to the Pacific Ocean to watch the giant waves crashing on the shore my wife and I decided we would move back to our home state of Missouri to enjoy our retirement. On a recent visit to my childhood neighborhood in northwest Missouri we drove through the entire area observing how life has changed since the 1920s.

The very small printing shop where Grandfather Cover published the *New Hampton Tribune* weekly newspaper still stands, but there has been no *Tribune* publication for decades. Walking around the outside of that building brought back memories of when I would spend time in that little shop as a five to ten year old. I was learning the journalism profession at a very early age.

Neighborhoods in my original home area have changed. In Martinsville, there are now only a few fine homes. The old brick building where I attended high school was still standing on a recent visit, but it has been vacant for decades. There are now no shops or stores in town. The Methodist church where I attended every Sunday and where my father was superintendent and my mother the pianist remains as a fine well maintained church.

There are far fewer country homes now than when I was a farm boy. Farms are much larger than when I was growing up on our family farm in the 1940s. Farm equipment of today is more modern, just as the automobiles of today bear no resemblance to those we drove in the 1930s. Life has definitely changed since I was a youngster.

Touring my boyhood neighborhood brought back precious memories of my early years on the farm in the 1930s. My old neighborhood is completely different now. There are no buildings on the farm that was my home from second grade through college. Likewise, many other former nearby houses and farm buildings no longer exist.

Rural America is much different today than it was in my years as a youngster on our farm in the 1930s and 1940s. Now if you live in a rural or small-town area just a quick comfortable drive in your fine automobile will get you to the larger towns or cities of the area for shopping or a visit with relatives and friends.

We have immediate communication with relatives or friends throughout the country. With cell phone we can now make immediate contact with a relative or friend down the road who may be expecting your visit and let them know if you have an unexpected delay. You can just as quickly dial the number of a relative or friend elsewhere in the United States. This was not even dreamed of when I was a farm boy in the 1930s and 1940s. Back then, you'd go to the telephone on the wall and twist the little handle on the side around and around to call a nearby neighbor who was on "your line." You had to call the telephone central office in a very nearby town for assistance in making a call just a relatively few miles away.

My wife and I now have family and friends scattered far and wide across the United States. We have grandchildren and great-grandchildren. I continue as an active member of the Optimist International organization. I have traveled to the East Coast to wade into the Atlantic Ocean. I have sat on the beaches of the West Coast and watched the giant waves come crashing on shore. We've enjoyed trips into Canada to the north and Mexico to the south.

There's a world of difference between life in America at the time of the arrival of my ancestors on the Mayflower in 1620 and what we experience today. Even in my own life since the early 1930s there have been constantly changing developments including the immediate verbalized and pictured television news right in the comfort of our home. I am grateful to all who have contributed significantly to the safety and security of this great land of ours.

THE END

Printed in the United States
By Bookmasters